FORAGING CENTRAL GRASSLANDS

HELP US KEEP THIS GUIDE UP TO DATE

Every effort has been made by the author and editors to make this guide as accurate and useful as possible. However, many things can change after a guide is published—regulations change, facilities come under new management, and so forth.

We would love to hear from you concerning your experiences with this guide and how you feel it could be improved and kept up to date. While we may not be able to respond to all comments and suggestions, we'll take them to heart, and we'll also make certain to share them with the author. Please send your comments and suggestions to falconeditorial@rowman.com.

Thanks for your input!

FORAGING CENTRAL GRASSLANDS

Finding, Identifying, and Preparing Edible Wild Foods
in the Central United States

Bo Brown

ESSEX, CONNECTICUT

FALCONGUIDES®

An imprint of Globe Pequot, the trade division of
The Rowman & Littlefield Publishing Group, Inc.
4501 Forbes Blvd., Ste. 200
Lanham, MD 20706
www.rowman.com

Falcon and FalconGuides are registered trademarks and Make Adventure Your Story
is a trademark of The Rowman & Littlefield Publishing Group, Inc.

Distributed by NATIONAL BOOK NETWORK

Photos by Bo Brown unless noted otherwise.
Maps by The Rowman & Littlefield Publishing Group, Inc.

British Library Cataloguing in Publication Information available

Library of Congress Cataloging-in-Publication Data available
ISBN 978-1-4930-6407-6 (paper: alk. paper)
ISBN 978-1-4930-6408-3 (electronic)

∞™ The paper used in this publication meets the minimum requirements of American National Standard
for Information Sciences—Permanence of Paper for Printed Library Materials, ANSI/NISO Z39.48-1992.

The author and The Rowman & Littlefield Publishing Group, Inc., assume no liability for accidents
happening to, or injuries sustained by, readers who engage in the activities described in this book.

This book is a work of reference. Readers should always consult an expert before using any foraged item. The author, editors, and publisher of this work have checked with sources believed to be reliable in their efforts to confirm the accuracy and completeness of the information presented herein and that the information is in accordance with the standard practices accepted at the time of publication. However, neither the author, editors, and publisher, nor any other party involved in the creation and publication of this work, warrant that the information is in every respect accurate and complete, and they are not responsible for errors or omissions or for any consequences from the application of the information in this book. In light of ongoing research and changes in clinical experience and in governmental regulations, readers are encouraged to confirm the information contained herein with additional sources. This book does not purport to be a complete presentation of all plants, and the genera, species, and cultivars discussed or pictured herein are but a small fraction of the plants found in the wild, in an urban or suburban landscape, or in a home. Given the global movement of plants, we would expect continual introduction of species having toxic properties to the regions discussed in this book. We have made every attempt to be botanically accurate, but regional variations in plant names, growing conditions, and availability may affect the accuracy of the information provided. A positive identification of an individual plant is most likely when a freshly collected part of the plant containing leaves and flowers or fruits is presented to a knowledgeable botanist or horticulturist. Poison Control Centers generally have relationships with the botanical community should the need for plant identification arise. We have attempted to provide accurate descriptions of plants, but there is no substitute for direct interaction with a trained botanist or horticulturist for plant identification.

In cases of exposure or ingestion, contact a Poison Control Center (1-800-222-1222), a medical toxicologist, another appropriate health-care provider, or an appropriate reference resource.

CONTENTS

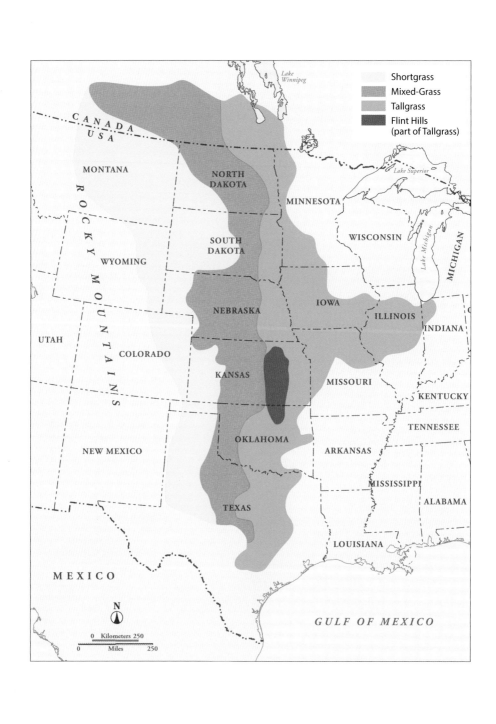

	Shortgrass
	Mixed-Grass
	Tallgrass
	Flint Hills (part of Tallgrass)

CANADA
USA

MONTANA

NORTH DAKOTA

MINNESOTA

Lake Superior

Lake Winnipeg

R O C K Y   M O U N T A I N S

WYOMING

SOUTH DAKOTA

WISCONSIN

Lake Michigan

MICHIGAN

UTAH

COLORADO

NEBRASKA

IOWA

ILLINOIS

INDIANA

KANSAS

MISSOURI

KENTUCKY

NEW MEXICO

OKLAHOMA

ARKANSAS

TENNESSEE

MISSISSIPPI

ALABAMA

TEXAS

LOUISIANA

MEXICO

N

GULF OF MEXICO

0   Kilometers   250
0   Miles   250

ACKNOWLEDGMENTS

My mom always gets top billing; she raised me on a riverbank and taught me how to fish, hunt, and gather her favorite wild greens for the dinner table. This instilled a lifelong love and passion for the outdoors, and I will be forever grateful to **Parthenia Jane Brown** for allowing me to grow up as a wild woods kid.

Chief Jim Fire Eagle Boose and bandmate/backpacking buddy **Don Brink** were critical influences in my life of teaching outdoor skills and songbird research. Fire Eagle was demonstrating flint knapping and plant lore at the Branson theme park Silver Dollar City in 1977 while I was a hired musician there. Don and I spent hours soaking up his knowledge of ancient ways, and the discovery of outdoor skills books by Larry Dean Olsen and Tom Brown Jr. turned our backpack trips into bushcraft practice sessions. Don also introduced me to birding, and I literally fell into a life of traveling the country to work on songbird studies. Fire Eagle's quote "All knowledge is incomplete till it's passed on" seemed like a good rule to live by. It led to both of us having careers in teaching and working in nature.

Singer/songwriter/storyteller/author and bandmate **Marideth Sisco** bugged me for years to write a book. Her persistence worked; she continues to be a source of assistance and inspiration on book two.

Thanks to bandmate **Emily Higgins** for mad proofing skills and her beautiful nature-based music that helps keep me sane.

Dr. Kitty Ledbetter provided critical assistance and a crash course in the rules of writing structure. I barely graduated high school, with no college or writing courses, and just hope some of it stuck.

Denise Thomas provided steadfast encouragement, proofreading, and writing tips; thanks for being my best cheerleader.

Dr. Kim Smith and **Dr. Jane Fitzgerald** (University of Arkansas, Fayetteville) hired this unqualified but highly enthusiastic nature geek in 1985 for my first songbird research job, an adventure that still continues today. That work provided an opportunity to learn volumes from people who knew far more than I ever would about the natural sciences.

A new generation now carries the torch—local foraging educator Rachel Elizabeth (*Eating the Ozarks*), permaculture homesteader/writer Wren Haffner (*Mountain Jewel*), Alexis Nikole Nelson (TikTok's "The Black Forager"), urban forager/gardener Indy Srnath, and others are building social media empires based on foraging and wild food. These encouraging signs, and social media posts of a 5-year-old boy making recipes from my first book, give me much hope that young people will continue the tradition.

My dog-eared books by Euell Gibbons, Bradford Angier, the Foxfire Book series, Tom Brown Jr., Billy Jo Tatum, and regional wildflower identification guides by Edgar Denison and Don Kurz all provided fodder for my early obsession with plants. Samuel Thayer, Christopher Nyerges, Green Deane, Pascal Baudar, Alan Bergo, and others continue to provide inspiration and push the boundaries.

Lastly, we owe a tremendous debt of gratitude to the original inhabitants of this country. They developed an intimate understanding of nature over millennia and passed it down through generations. We are beneficiaries of that knowledge, and sadly, did not always repay the favor with kindness. Learning the ancient foodways and rehabilitating land back into wild food forests and prairies will benefit our health, the environment, and our enjoyment of nature.

Native Americans authors and writers like Linda Black Elk, Sean Sherman (*The Sioux Chef*), and many others are currently creating and teaching about new cuisines based on traditional foodways, and recent popular books like *Braiding Sweetgrass* (Robin Wall Kemmerer), *Tending the Wild* (M. Kat Anderson), and others are showing that we still have much to learn from indigenous peoples about our relationship with the earth.

INTRODUCTION

This book is intended to be an easy-to-use field reference for both beginning and seasoned foragers to aid in finding, identifying, and preparing the wealth of wild edible plants found in the central grasslands and surrounding landscapes. There is always a choice to be made in these works: cover a small number of plants in great depth or include as many species as possible and cover each as thoroughly as is feasible given the size limitations of the book. I chose the latter because plant diversity in our diets is critical to good health, and it offers a wider range of culinary flavors when preparing your harvest. This book is not a complete accounting of edible plants found in the region; that work would require multiple volumes or a larger book than could accurately be called a field guide.

Foraging guides specific to grasslands are rare, but one caught my attention. *Edible Wild Plants of the Prairie: An Ethnobotanical Guide* (Dr. Kelly Kindscher, 1987) described prairie food plants the author encountered during a 700-mile, eighty-day walk from the mouth of the Kansas River to the outskirts of Denver. It was the first guide I'd seen of its type and contained a wealth of information about indigenous people's names, uses, and preparation of wild food plants. When Falcon Guides offered me another title after the release of my first book, *Foraging the Ozarks*, Dr. Kindscher provided invaluable insights and his book served as an inspiration for this work.

A reason for a lack of grassland-specific foraging books may be that unbroken-sod tallgrass and mixed-grass prairies are a globally endangered habitat today, and much of what original prairie remains is in private or public preserves scattered throughout ten states (see "The Central Grasslands Physiographic Region"). Most of these preserves do not allow collecting, but many food plants found there also occur in various other habitats in the surrounding regions. The region provides ample foraging opportunities in both natural and human-altered landscapes.

THE "WHY" OF FORAGING (BESIDES FREE FOOD!)

We've become a fast-food nation, putting convenience over quality to the detriment of our health. Embrace slow food. Real food. You literally are what you eat, and wild food is medicine. Decades of studies show that wild plants are consistently more nutrient-dense and vitamin-rich than domesticated plants. They also contain many beneficial medicinal compounds such as anthocyanins, polyphenols, and other phytonutrients, minerals, and trace elements. Simply adding foraged foods to your existing diet can help make up for the nutritional and medicinal shortcomings of our commercial food supply while providing a bounty of flavor combinations not found on market shelves. Empty grocery shelves during the COVID-19 pandemic reminded people of the fact that our food supply can easily be disrupted. A connection to the land, our food, and where it comes from may at any time become a critical survival skill.

My first deep dive into foraging was originally rooted in wilderness survival, to learn what could be eaten during long backpack trips and outings. This came in handy later during bird research fieldwork in isolated areas without regular opportunities to buy groceries; foraged food helped keep me fed in those situations. During the last couple of decades, my focus and passion has shifted to the culinary possibilities, and it is a very exciting prospect to discover all the different flavors and preparation methods possible. Books by Pascal Baudar, Alan Bergo, Sean Sherman, and others have introduced many new food concepts and ideas, and social media foraging sites feature people experimenting with new creations on their own. I've had a good basic knowledge of local plants for decades, but nearly every week I discover new edible parts or new preparations of plants I've known my entire life. It's a great time to be alive as a forager!

ORGANIZATION AND SCOPE OF THIS BOOK

A handy reference list of plants by food type (e.g., fruits/berries, seeds, greens, roots, etc.) can be found in Appendix A.

Tips on collection, preparation, processing, and use of the various species covered can be found in Appendix B: Getting Started.

Plants are grouped into general classes (clades) of Eudicots and Monocots, listed by their Latin family names in alphabetical order. Common names, genus/species, habitat, and range are included in the listings. When plants have several common names, the Native American name for the plant is preferable when in widespread usage. A general understanding of plant families will aid in learning characteristics common to each. This knowledge will help in recognizing new plants when located out of context and will hopefully lead to better overall identification skills.

Native and introduced species found in the historic range of tallgrass and mixed-grass prairie are covered. This area encompasses various types of original and reclaimed prairies, prairie transitional zones, midwestern oak savannahs, prairie wetlands, ponds/potholes, wooded riparian areas, croplands and their borders, and human-altered habitats in the surrounding regions. Some species are not commonly referenced in other foraging resources; others are well-known. Some plants may be found in much of the covered range, while others may be restricted to parts of one or two states.

Each plant entry features a detailed description written in field-guide style, color photos with some plants in various growth stages, and collection/preparation tips with recipes. Proper identification is key When you know a plant's name, you can learn what the rest of the world knows about it. **Points of critical**

interest are highlighted in bold type. Botanical terms are used for brevity's sake; a glossary of terms is included at the back of the book. Most plant species were selected for their ability to provide food throughout the different seasons; others were chosen for their interesting flavors or seasonings in culinary and beverage use. A few uncommon prairie plants were included to promote conservation efforts related to the species. Field-expedient medicinal and utilitarian uses are included, but most entries mention general medicinal use only to encourage further study for those so inclined. **Toxic look-alikes, cautions, and similar edible species are explained in the "Warnings/Comments" section.** The chapter on poisonous plants covers species that could be potentially fatal if ingested or could cause severe contact dermatitis if touched. Mushrooms were excluded from the book, as existing publications dedicated solely to fungi cover the subject in finer detail than could be included in this work. A brief segment on edible insects is provided in Appendix C.

GENERAL FORAGING GUIDELINES
Please read this part before beginning to forage!

Never consume wild plants unless you are 100 percent sure of identification and take the time to cross-reference your ID with other sources. Always practice safe, ethical, and sustainable collecting methods.

Never depend on a single source when identifying unfamiliar plants. Relying solely on plant ID phone apps or foraging/edible plant groups on social media can lead to unpleasant or even disastrous experiences. I've witnessed numerous instances of toxic or dangerous plants misidentified as edible on those sources.

Legality
All public lands, roadsides, and waterways have regulations for collecting plants, and the rules are varied: Digging roots, bulbs, and tubers are generally prohibited on all public land; always check local regulations. Private landowners and farmers often allow collection of wild foods and some root harvesting with permission; always ask first.

Although federal and state lands prohibit digging roots, many allow collection of greens, fruits, berries, nuts, and mushrooms for personal consumption. Some areas allow collection only with a permit, issued at the supervisor's discretion. Some public parks may ban all collection except what is eaten within the park. Always check first before collecting, as fines for prohibited activities can be quite steep.

Ethical Collecting
Plant names are listed with "native," "introduced," or other descriptions in the first heading to provide an indication as to how much, or whether to harvest.

Many introduced plants are widespread or invasive in a wide range of habitats and can be collected in volume without consequence. The "invasivore" movement is becoming popular in some areas, where foragers collect only nonnative invasive plants or animals for food to help mitigate possible environmental and economic damages they may cause. Native plants are often more restricted in range and to specific habitats; please protect any plant's ability to reproduce by collecting reproductive parts, whole shoots, or roots only when found in abundance. Spread out your collecting activities over a large area, and when collecting bulbs or roots from colonies, don't take them all from one spot; a bit of thinning can improve the vigor and life of a colony over time.

The region is home to several iconic wild food species still used by the Lakota and other tribes, with common names like biscuitroot (*šahíyela*), breadroot/prairie turnip (*thíŋpsila*), and chokecherry (*Čhaŋpȟá*). Indigenous peoples' main food source prior to European contact were large herbivores such as bison, elk, deer, and pronghorn, but knowledge of these plants and others was critical to their health and survival.

A few species requiring optimal prairie conditions have become uncommon due to habitat loss. Regenerative management regimens featuring short-duration rotational grazing, prescribed burns, and planting/seeding of native species are having success in reestablishing these endangered habitats. Promoting the propagation and cultivation of less common natives in suitable habitats and gardens may serve to supplement wild populations. Several species are also beautiful wildflowers with edible roots or tubers, so thoughtful consideration and attention to legality is required on whether to harvest such plants in the wild.

A good rule is to take no more than 15 to 20 percent of root plants that are present.

Help increase the population of less common desirable natives by collecting seeds when present, or use viable seeds left over after processing to start new populations in nearby suitable habitats or flower gardens. Several invasive and environmentally damaging species are listed in this book; avoid distributing those seeds or viable plant parts into new areas.

Always set an example with your collecting habits. The more people see best practices and good stewardship in foraging, the less apt they will be to view it as a destructive activity. Pass on your knowledge of these things whenever possible; you'll learn more by teaching what you know.

Sustainable Harvesting Tips

Taproots—Extract the taproot and rootlets with the top attached, cut the top of the root about ¾-inch or so from the green top, and replant the top and bit of taproot upright into the dug-up ground. If collected at the flowering stage, replanting the top and bit of taproot into the dug ground will often allow flowers to mature and drop seeds. These seeds are more likely to germinate than those dropped on compacted soil.

Shoots—Most plants will produce another shoot when the original is taken, but some do not. Always leave plenty to allow reproduction.

Bulbs—Remove any small bulblets attached to the main bulb and deposit them in the dug-up ground.

Tubers—Take a few but leave the smaller ones. With larger tubers such as wild potato, only take a bit of the root and leave or replant the rest; it will continue to grow. If ripe fruits or seeds are present, deposit them in the dug-up ground, or replant them in other likely habitats.

Greens—Collect only the tender leaves and tops and leave what you won't use.

Plants have co-evolved with animals and insects that eat them and will counteract the stress of being eaten by producing more stems, foliage, reproductive parts, and seeds; this is called herbivory overcompensation. This growth stimulation can extend the collection period, but always leave enough to make seeds for future propagation. Always be aware of your impacts and make them positive whenever possible.

Health Concerns

Allergic reactions to certain plants: When consuming a new plant for the first time, try a small sample first and wait for a while to check for an unpleasant reaction. These reactions seem to be on the increase, many from exposure to common foods like peanuts and wheat. Pollution, less diversity in our diets, and less exposure to microbes in nature can change how our immune systems respond to what we eat. Increased nutrient intake, particularly nutrients associated with prevention of allergic diseases such as omega-3 fatty acids and non-digestible fibers are shown to reduce food allergies. A more diverse diet and exposure to different food allergens from an early age may lead to tolerance development and fewer allergies.

Don't consume large quantities of one type of wild plant. Wild plants are far more nutrient-dense and vitamin-rich than commercially available foods. They also contain much higher levels of various beneficial compounds, some of which may cause stomach distress when consumed in quantity. These compounds have been diluted in modern crops, so eating a plateful of broccoli or other garden vegetable isn't comparable to an equal amount of wild food in this respect.

Be aware of pollution. Plants collected from ditches, roadsides, edges of pastures, or near agricultural fields may be susceptible to pollution by herbicide/pesticide spraying and heavy metals accumulation in agricultural run-off. These dangers are present but may be somewhat over-hyped; studies have shown that many plants collected in urban and other suspect habitats don't present a hazard after being rinsed in tap water and tested. Below is an excerpt from an article by the National Institutes of Health National Library of Medicine, titled "Open-source food: Nutrition, toxicology, and availability of wild edible greens in the East Bay."

> *Wild edible greens harvested in industrial, mixed-use, and high-traffic urban areas in the San Francisco East Bay area are abundant and highly nutritious. Even grown in soils with elevated levels of heavy metals, tested species were safe to eat after rinsing in tap water. This does not mean that all edible greens growing in contaminated soil are safe to eat—tests on more species, in more locations, and over a broader range of soil chemistry are needed to determine what is generally safe and what is not. But it does suggest that wild greens could contribute to nutrition, food security, and sustainability in urban ecosystems. Current laws, regulations, and public-health guidance that forbid or discourage foraging on public lands, including urban areas, should be revisited.*

THE CENTRAL GRASSLANDS PHYSIOGRAPHIC REGION

The area occupies a swath from northeastern Texas to the Dakotas and parts of Oklahoma, Kansas, Missouri, Nebraska, Iowa, Illinois, Iowa, and Minnesota, with distinct habitat differences occurring in the Osage Plains, Flint Hills, Blackland Prairies, Cross Timbers, and Coteau des Prairies.

The region is dotted with prairie preserves as small as a few dozen acres and as large as several thousand acres. The largest remaining unplowed area of tallgrass prairie is the 4-million-acre, 60-mile swath of the Kansas Flint Hills. It consists of rolling, sloping plains and low hills underlain with limestone and/or sandstone bedrock, and runs from northern Oklahoma to the Nebraska border. The 70,000-acre Sheyenne National Grassland near Lisbon, North Dakota, and the 40,000-acre Joseph H. Williams Tallgrass Prairie Reserve near Pawhuska, Oklahoma, are believed to be the largest preserves outside the Flint Hills.

The moisture gradient between the humid East and the arid West delineates the grasslands into roughly three narrow zones: the tallgrass prairie and prairie transitional areas that abut the Ozarks and eastern deciduous forests to the east, the midwestern mixed-grass prairie, and the western shortgrass prairie to the west that is typified by low and irregular precipitation with periodic drought. Shortgrass prairie is typically a graminoid-dominant habitat with a less diverse plant community and is not thoroughly covered in this work.

The topography is relatively level, but relief is present in the form of scattered rolling hills, breaks, salt plains, low mountains, gypsum buttes, sandy flats, and sand dunes; the north tends to be less flat than the south. Most prairie soils tend to be deep, fertile, dark, and mostly free of rocks, and are sought for their high crop productivity. Soil color ranges from black in more mesic areas to brown or yellowish brown in semiarid areas. These soils support amazing floral and faunal diversity: A square yard of tallgrass soil to a depth of 51 centimeters may contain over 110,000 arthropods and 5.4 million nematodes.

The major rivers include the Red River, Platte River, Missouri River, Arkansas River, and Mississippi River. These rivers may have seasonal high flows in late spring/early summer following spring runoff and much lower flows in late summer/early autumn. This fluctuation allows development of ephemeral habitats including sandbars, mudflats, gravel bars, and diverse successional understory flora in riparian forests.

History

The great American prairie was the largest continuous ecosystem on the continent before the European settlers arrived. It extended in an unbroken swath between Texas and Canada and was home to one of the largest ungulate herds (bison) in the world. Often referred to as the Great American Desert and the American Serengeti, the Great Plains of North America occupy approximately 502,000 square miles. Comparatively, the Serengeti of Africa covers about 12,000 square miles.

Indigenous cultures occupied the Great Plains and Canadian Prairies region for thousands of years prior to European contact. Some were nomadic hunter-gatherers; some became sedentary or semi-sedentary farmers. The region is known for the horse cultures that flourished from the seventeenth century through the late nineteenth century. Their nomadism and armed resistance to domination by the military forces of the United States and Canada have made the Plains Indian an archetype in art and literature for Native Americans everywhere, however inaccurate that may be.

European immigrants on their westward journeys found the fertile prairie soils to be excellent for crop production. With the help of John Deere's steel moldboard plow, they turned the diverse prairies into agricultural land. Today, most of our original prairies have long been converted to crop- or pastureland. The Kansas Flint Hills and Coteau des Prairies in northeastern North Dakota escaped the plow because of rocky topography, leading to the prevalence of cattle ranches instead of croplands more typical of soil prairies. These ranches occasionally rely on annual controlled burns to renew the prairie grasses and forbs for cattle grazing, but most are too heavily grazed to support the original native flora. Some ranches are being successfully managed in conjunction with prairie preservation/restoration organizations and regenerative agriculturists to reestablish or preserve the original habitats.

POISONOUS PLANTS

Below is a list of plants that may be confused with edible species and that contain dangerous to potentially fatal toxin levels if ingested. Poison ivy and its relatives, and some members of the family *Apiaceae* (carrots), such as wild parsnips, contain oils that can cause a severe dermatitis rash. There are other toxic plants present, but these are the most dangerous if consumed by mistake. Several plants listed in this book have edible fruits when ripe, but unripe fruits and other parts may be toxic. Ground plum, ground cherry, and elderberry fall into this category. Some plants need to be boiled to cook off the toxins, such as pokeweed.

EASTERN DEATH CAMAS
Toxicoscordion nuttallii
Family: Melanthiaceae, native

Death camas contains the neurotoxic alkaloids zygacine and zygadenine. This showy perennial emerges from a bulb as a basal rosette of 6–10 erect, linear leaves surrounded by a papery sheath at the base. As the central flowering stem emerges, the leaves grow up to 15" long and ¾" wide, becoming thick, stout, and arching. The smooth stem forms as a raceme with cream-white flowers about ½" across. It is somewhat similar in structure and appearance to the edible wild hyacinth (*Camassia scilloides*), but is generally stouter in appearance, and its flower petals are white, shorter, broader, and on longer stalks. The bulbs of the two plants may be difficult to differentiate. **If collecting wild hyacinth, identify the plants while in the flowering stage to make sure the entire colony is the same species and doesn't have death camas growing within it.**

POISON HEMLOCK
Conium maculatum
Family: Apiaceae, introduced

DJTANNG, WIKIMEDIA COMMONS

Poison hemlock is a vigorous and aggressive biennial that emerges from a taproot as a basal rosette. Compound basal leaves are up to 12" long and 12" across and are generally triangular. Leaflets are double or triple bipinnately compound, with a lacy appearance. The second-year flowering stem is up to 8' tall, with longitudinal veins that give it a ribbed appearance. The stem is smooth and hollow, with purple spots on the lower half and a whitish bloom on the surface that easily wipes off; it develops alternate leaves that become smaller as they ascend the stem. Small, white flowers emerge in midsummer, forming on loosely clustered, rounded umbels at the stem and branch terminus. The mature taproot and all plant parts have a generally disagreeable smell. Emerging young basal leaves of poison hemlock appear generally thicker and more robust when compared with the sparser and generally hairy foliage of wild carrot (*D. carota*). Carrot roots will always have the characteristic carrot odor. All parts of poison hemlock contain the toxin coniine, which has a chemical structure resembling nicotine; the taproot contains the highest concentration. This toxin disrupts the central nervous system, and even a small dose may cause respiratory collapse and death. Some develop contact dermatitis from touching it.

WATER HEMLOCK (AKA SPOTTED COWBANE)
Cicuta maculata
Family: Apiaceae, native

Water hemlock's flower structure and general plant structure is similar to poison hemlock, but its leaves are linear instead of fernlike. Its hollow, flowering stems are up to 6' tall, smooth, green to purplish, often with longitudinal veins. Compound leaves are up to 1' long, odd-pinnate or doubly odd-pinnate; leaflets are up to 4" long and 1¼" wide, linear or lanceolate to ovate-elliptic, often with coarsely toothed margins. Its mature taproot contains hollow chambers. All parts of the plant contain cicutoxin, a highly poisonous unsaturated alcohol with a strong odor. The toxin is found principally in the taproot but is also present in the leaves and stems during early growth. Water hemlock has been mistakenly identified as similar edible species such as wild parsnip and has caused fatalities. Some sources suggest avoidance of all plants in the family Apiaceae with a similar appearance until their physical characteristics are fully understood and positive identification is absolute.

POISON IVY, POISON OAK
Toxicodendron radicans, T. rydbergii, T. pubescens
Family: Anacardiaceae, native

Poison ivy is common and rampant in many parts of the country. This extremely variable plant can appear as a ground cover, a low upright shrub to 5', or a small to large woody vine over 4" in diameter that climbs trees up to 60'. It has alternate, trifoliate leaves on long, slender petioles; the center leaflet is always on a longer stalk than the two lateral leaflets. The blade surface can be dull or shiny, with margins that are entire, lobed, or broadly and sparsely toothed. The vines are attached to trees or other substrates by hairlike aerial rootlets. Sparse panicles of small, yellowish-white flowers form across from the leaf axils. Fruits are green, round drupes about ¼" across that mature to white. Southern poison oak (*T. pubescens*) is similar but with more rounded leaflets and tends to grow as an upright shrub rather than a climbing vine.

Not everyone is affected by the urushiol oils, and some that have never had a reaction may become allergic at some point. If contact is suspected, scrub all parts of the skin that may have been exposed with Dawn soap and cold water within an hour or two, even areas not initially exposed. The oil is persistent and can remain on dead vines, clothing, gloves, and tools for a long time. It spreads easily and can be transferred to your skin from your clothing when removing them, or even by petting your dog or cat after it has been exposed. If a rash develops, several over-the-counter and prescription medicines are available. Effective wild plant medicines (in poultices and tinctures) are jewelweed (*Impatiens* spp.) and broad-leaved plantain (*Plantago* spp.).

Eudicots

Eudicots (formerly Dicots) are classified as flowering plants having two cotyledons in the seed, leaves with a network of veins radiating from a central main vein, flower parts in multiples of four or five, and a taproot or similar root system.

ADOXACEAE (MUSKROOTS, ELDERBERRIES, VIBURNUMS, MOSCHATELS)

A small family of flowering plants consisting of five genera and about 150 to 200 species, including both woody-stemmed and herbaceous species. Most have flat-topped inflorescences composed of numerous small flowers that mature to produce fleshy drupes.

COMMON ELDERBERRY
Sambucus canadensis and others

Edible parts/harvest time: Berries, only when ripe in mid- to late summer. Unripe berries, stems, and foliage may be toxic. Native.

Elderberry is a true superfood highly sought after by the health food market for its immune system support and antioxidant and nutritional properties. Recent studies confirm that compounds from elderberry concentrate can directly inhibit the flu virus entry and replication in human cells.

Description: A deciduous, colony-forming shrub up to 10' tall, often with multiple, arching stems that branch toward the top. Older stems have rough, grayish-brown bark with large, raised lenticels. Branches and twigs are grayish to yellowish brown, often smooth but occasionally ridged, with sparse lenticels. Young stems can be weak and brittle due to the prominent pith center. Shiny, dark green opposite leaves grow along stems and branches, each is 6–12" long, odd-pinnately compound, with 2–4 opposite pairs of leaflets and one terminal leaflet. Leaflets are lanceolate to ovoid, 2–6" long, 1–2" wide, with serrated margins. Flat or dome-shaped, snowy-white flower clusters up to 10" across form in late May–July, emerging on umbel-like panicles at the tips of branches; individual ¼" flowers are 4 petaled. Fruiting heads mature in August–October to bear numerous shiny, purplish-black round berries that are ¼" across, each containing 4 seeds.

Red elderberry (*S. racemosa*) is similar but has red berries; it is found throughout the western United States, and from Minnesota throughout the Northeast to Maine.

Habitat/Range: Occurs in prairies, pastures, old shelterbelts, overgrown meadows, abandoned farmsteads, gardens, thickets, fencerows, bottomland forests and borders, streambanks, borders of ponds and lakes, seeps, ditches, and along roadsides, railroads, and power line cuts. Range is throughout most of the eastern and western states. Mostly absent from a swath of drier habitats in the shortgrass prairie region from Texas to Canada.

Uses: Ripe berries are edible raw, but flavor is improved by lightly cooking or drying. The processed berries are great for syrup, jelly, wine, and brandy, and can be used in pies and other confections. Dried berries can be added to pancakes, sweet breads, muffins, and other sweet dishes. Fresh flowers are good fresh or dried for tea or can be fermented to make Elderflower Champagne. Add them to breads, pancakes, and salads, or fry whole flower heads in a light batter as fritters. Use only the flowers and remove as many stems

Elderberry in bloom, with ripe fruits

as possible. To harvest berries, collect the whole fruiting heads and freeze, then shake over a tarp or newspapers to easily remove berries from stems, or use a large-toothed comb to remove them. Soak in water to remove leftover stems, debris, and unripe berries. Various parts of the plant are used as internal or external medicine to treat numerous ailments.

Warnings/Comments: The root, stems, leaves, and unripe berries contain toxic cyanide-forming glycosides. Consume only ripe berries; remove stems and unripe berries when processing. Several cultivar species with higher fruit yields are planted commercially.

RECIPE

ELDERFLOWER CHAMPAGNE

12–16 medium to large elderberry flower heads

4 cups white sugar

1 gallon cold water

2–3 lemons, juiced, their skins zested or quartered

2–3 tablespoons white wine vinegar

1. Remove flowers from stems.

2. Dissolve sugar in a container with a bit of the water, heated to warm.

3. Mix the dissolved sugar with the other ingredients and the remaining water in a large, covered crock. Leave covered in a cool place for 2–3 days; stir gently several times a day. Natural yeast on the flowers should create fermentation; if signs aren't present after a couple of days, add a bit of champagne yeast.

4. Strain and pour into clean screw-top or swing-top glass bottles; leave in a dark place at ambient room temperature for another 4–10 days. Test every 2 days or so to make sure the mixture isn't over-carbonated by gently unscrewing the lids to let gases escape. The bottles may explode if left unattended too long; putting them in lidded buckets will help avoid messes. *Note:* Cooler environments may require more time to ferment, as the natural yeast in the flowers may take awhile to get going. The longer the champagne ferments, the higher the alcohol content.

5. When alcohol content and carbonation level reach your preference, refrigerate to slow further fermentation.

AMARANTHACEAE (AMARANTHS, GOOSEFOOTS)

A large family of worldwide-distributed herbs and shrubs, consisting of roughly 2,040 species in 165 genera. It includes the former goosefoot family (Chenopodiaceae) making it the most species-rich lineage within its parent order, Caryophyllales. Some members are economically important food crops such as beets and quinoa, and many are cultivated as garden ornamentals.

COMMON AMARANTH (AKA REDROOT, ROUGH PIGWEED)
Amaranthus retroflexus and others

Edible parts/harvest time: Shoots in late spring. Tender tops in spring/summer. Seeds in late summer/fall. Native and introduced, potentially invasive.

Amaranth seeds and greens are steeped in pre-Hispanic Mexican history and were diet staples in ancient Mesoamerica. The seed flour was predominant in Aztec culture and was fashioned into images of gods and eaten as communion. This led to the banning of its cultivation by Christian Europeans during their colonization of Mexico. It has recently become popular as a gluten-free and super-nutritious wheat alternative.

Description: Common amaranth is a weedy annual 1–3' tall, with a hairy, branched central stem terminating in bristly flower spikes. Alternate, simple leaves are ovate to elliptic, up to 6" long and 4" across, becoming smaller as they ascend the stem. The lower leaf surface is pubescent, the upper surface less so. Leaf margins are smooth or slightly wavy; veins appear as grooves. In late summer, the stems and branches produce a flowering panicle of bristly pale green or purple spikes up to 6" long, with shorter spikes forming at the leaf axil. As the spikes dry, they release prodigious amounts of tiny, flattened-roundish, tan or black seeds.

White amaranth (*A. albus*) has smaller leaves and whitish stems. Prostrate pigweed/matweed (*A. blitoides*) has branched prostrate stems emerging from a stout taproot, often forming large mats. Smooth, fleshy stems are up to 3' long and may vary in color from pale green to pale red. Its shiny, alternate leaves are elliptic, obovate or oval, with smooth margins; they are generally smaller than on other amaranths. Many amaranth cultivars have

Prostrate pigweed

been developed, some for ornamental gardens and some that produce larger, white seeds for commercial sale and consumption. **Habitat/Range:** Prefers disturbed, open habitats. Found in gardens, barnyards, pastures, croplands, old fields, roadsides, and waste areas. Many species occurring in the United States are native to the tropical Americas and have naturalized throughout the United States and Canada. Amaranths are widely cultivated for culinary and ornamental uses throughout Eurasia and Africa.

Uses: Young shoots, tender tops, and leaves can be added raw to salads or cooked as a potherb. (See "Warnings" about consuming raw amaranth.) Use greens as you would its cousin, spinach. Cheera Thoran is a popular Indian dish combining finely cut amaranth leaves with grated coconut, chili peppers, and spices. The nutritious seeds can be sprouted, cooked as a cereal, or popped and used in *alegria*, a confection with Aztec origins. Seeds can be roasted and ground into flour for making crackers, tortillas, muffins, cakes, and breads, or used to make beverages such as beer or *atole* (a warm beverage often made with corn masa). To harvest, twist and work the fully dried flower spikes inside a plastic bag to release the seeds, then winnow the remaining dried bracts by bowl-to-bowl (or hand-to-hand) pouring while blowing through it, or by pouring in front of a fan on low setting (too much air will also blow away the tiny seeds). A flour sifter can speed the process, as most of the seeds will fall through the wire mesh. What remains can be further bowl-winnowed till clean. Whole plants in the genera *Amaranthus*, *Chenopodium*, *Atriplex*, and other salt-tolerant species can be used to produce a local salt. The plants are dried and burned to white ash then added to water; the filtrate is then evaporated in a pot. The residue can be used as a salt substitute. This method also can be used to make salt with wood ash from nontoxic trees and their roots. All parts of amaranth species have been used for food and medicine since prehistoric times.

Warnings/Comments: *Amaranthus*, *Atriplex*, *Chenopodium*, and related species contain high levels of oxalic acid and should be avoided by those prone to kidney stones and related ailments. Cooking helps remove some but not all oxalates. Amaranths may become agricultural pests: Water hemp and Palmer amaranth produce hundreds of thousands of seeds per plant and are particularly problematic in croplands as herbicide-resistant strains develop.

Amaranth seedheads and seeds

CHEERA THORAN

2 bunches (2–3 cups) amaranth leaves, finely chopped (substitute lamb's quarter or spinach)

1 tablespoon oil

1 teaspoon mustard seeds

2 dried red chili peppers, finely chopped

1 medium onion, finely chopped

4–5 garlic cloves, finely chopped

½ teaspoon turmeric powder

Salt to taste

½ cup grated coconut

1. Wash amaranth leaves before chopping (use stems if they aren't fibrous)
2. Heat oil in a skillet; add mustard seeds and cook till they splutter. Add chilies, onion, and garlic and sauté till onions are translucent.
3. Add chopped amaranth leaves, turmeric powder, and salt. Cover and cook on low flame for 5–7 minutes.
4. Add grated coconut, mix, and remove from the flame. Serve with cooked rice.

RECIPE

ALEGRIA (SPANISH FOR HAPPINESS)

Popping the small wild seeds must be done carefully in small batches. It's a bit time-consuming, but happiness is worth the effort!

1 cup amaranth seeds (wild amaranth or commercial white amaranth)

2 tablespoons honey

1 tablespoon table or blackstrap molasses

Dash of cinnamon or similar spices

Optional: ½ cup toasted pepitas, chopped (or use chopped nuts and raisins)

1. Using a heavy-bottomed, lidded pan preheated to medium heat, add seeds ½–1 teaspoon at a time, cover immediately, and vigorously shake the pan back and forth. The seeds should start to pop quickly and increase in intensity over the next 10–15 seconds. If the pan is too hot, it will smell burned; toss those and start with a cooler pan. Remove from heat when the popping slows down. Clean out the pan with a small natural-fiber brush (nothing that will melt); otherwise the remaining seeds will burn and ruin the next batch. Repeat until you have roughly a heaping cup of popped seeds.

2. Boil the honey and molasses in a saucepan on medium-high heat for about 3 minutes until it thickens and become viscous, taking care not to burn it. When it drips slowly off a spoon, add dry ingredients and spices and mix well. While mixture is still hot, place on a sheet of parchment paper on a flat tray. Let cool just enough to touch, then spread the mixture evenly while pressing and compacting with another sheet of parchment to bind everything together. Let cool till it hardens, cut into bars, and serve. Alternately, form into small balls.

SALINE SALTBUSH (AKA HALBERD-LEAVED ORACH)
Atriplex subspicata and others

Edible parts/harvest time: Shoots and tops in late spring–midsummer. Seeds in late summer. Native.

Description: An annual herb 1–3' tall, with erect, angular, many-branched stems, usually with green to reddish stripes on the lower half. Lower leaves are opposite on long petioles, becoming alternate and nearly sessile as they ascend the stem. Leaf blades are somewhat fleshy. Upper leaves are lanceolate; lower leaves are oblong-ovate to triangulate, often with blunt lobes at the base. Margins are entire or with shallow, broad teeth. Flowers appear in June–August as monoecious clusters on stems emerging from the leaf axils. Small seeds develop inside leafy capsules.

Habitat/Range: Found in alkali or saline soils in prairies, pastures, ditches near cultivated fields, disturbed ground, road-sides, and waste areas near buildings. Occurs throughout the Great Plains and in scattered locations over much of the western and northern United States.

Uses: All aboveground parts have a somewhat salty, spinach-like flavor. Young leaves can be added to salads and cooked dishes or boiled as a potherb. Young shoots can be cooked as a vegetable. Seeds can be eaten raw, cooked, or dried and ground as a flour additive. Tops can be used to make wild salt (see common amaranth for the process).

Warnings/Comments: Most *Atriplex* species taste somewhat salty because they accumulate salt from the soil, but they may also accumulate the mineral selenium where present. Selenium is beneficial in small amounts but toxic in larger doses; it's best to minimize consumption when collecting from areas known for high-selenium soils. The genus includes many species, some herbaceous and some with woody stems. A few species are rare and found only in specialized habitats.

LAMB'S QUARTER (AKA GOOSEFOOT)
Chenopodium album and others

Edible parts/harvest time: Shoots and leaves in late spring to late summer, seeds in late summer to early fall. Introduced and native.

Spinach is the most well-known and widely cultivated member of this family. The seeds of a South American species have recently become popular as a gluten-free alternative to wheat, sold commercially as the Incan grain quinoa.

Description: *C. album* is a weedy annual 1–6' tall, usually branched, with a bushy appearance. Stem is smooth and angular, pale green, developing purplish linear stripes with age. Alternate leaves are varied, up to 5" long and 3" wide, either diamond-shaped, triangular, or lanceolate, with lobed or dentate margins on larger leaves. Leaf undersides and young stems have a white, mealy coating. Minute, green flowers form in small clusters along spikes at leaf axils and the end of stems, sometimes becoming reddish at maturity. The ovary of each flower produces a flattened, somewhat round, black seed; one plant can produce up to 75,000 seeds.

The native pitseed goosefoot (*C. berlandieri*) has a similar stem structure but with more dense, larger seed clusters and narrower leaves with serrated margins. Several species have narrower, mostly unlobed leaves, or larger leaves may have 1 or 2 lobes. Maple-leaved goosefoot (*C. simplex*) has a less weedy appearance than others in the genus,

Pitseed goosefoot

rarely growing over 3' tall. Its ovate or deltoid-ovate leaves are up to 6" long and 4" across with large, widely spaced and pointed teeth and a general maple-leaved appearance. Most *Chenopodium* species have the characteristic white mealy substance on the top leaves and blade undersurface and will tolerate sandy or salty habitats. The white substance is somewhat salty to the taste, an indication of its ability to mine salt and other minerals from the soil.

Habitat/Range: A disturbed-ground species found in mostly open habitats, edges of prairies, pastures, cropland, gardens, old fields, vacant lots, and waste areas. Occurs throughout North America. *C. album* was first thought to have originated in Eurasia, but pre-contact archaeological remains have been found in the Americas; its origins are unclear.

Uses: Young, raw leaves are excellent in salads, and older leaves can be boiled, steamed, and used in soups or other cooked dishes. Use any way you would use spinach. The seeds can be dried and ground into flour or added to other plant seeds such as curly dock, amaranth, or climbing buckwheat to make crackers or seedcakes. The entire plant can be pulled when seeds are ripe and hung upside down to dry. When thoroughly dried, strip the foliage and seeds for use in soups and other cooked dishes, or grind for use as a flour additive or soup thickener.

Warnings/Comments: Plants in this family contain high amounts of oxalic acid and should be consumed sparingly or avoided entirely by those suffering from kidney stones and related ailments. Pitseed goosefoot and others have a long history of use and cultivation by indigenous Americans. Many species readily hybridize; several species have naturalized globally due to anthropogenic distribution and cultivation.

RECIPE

WILD SEED CRACKERS

¼ cup wild seeds (lamb's quarter, curly dock, plantain, evening primrose, amaranth, etc.), crushed or processed

1½ cups blanched almond flour

¼ cup ground flax meal

1–2 tablespoons finely chopped fresh horseweed, wild bergamot leaves, wild carrot, or other nontoxic seeds for seasoning (substitute rosemary or your favorite savory herbs)

1 egg white

Sea salt and pepper to taste

1. Preheat oven to 325°F. Mix all ingredients together by hand; if the dough is a bit dry, add 1 teaspoon of water at a time until the mix holds together.

2. When everything is well mixed and sticking together, form into a ball and transfer onto a piece of parchment paper. Press the dough down to flatten it, then cover with a second piece of parchment paper and roll out the dough uniformly to the desired thickness. If the sides crack apart, just push them back together. Carefully transfer the rolled cracker onto a large cookie sheet. Score with a pizza cutter into small squares, then sprinkle the tops of the crackers with a coarse sea salt and pepper.

3. Bake for 20 minutes until light browning occurs. If the cracker is still soft, bake in 5-minute increments until it firms a bit, but avoid burning it. Allow to cool on the baking sheet; it will firm up and become crispy once cool. When cool, break into pieces and store in an airtight container.

ANACARDIACEAE (CASHEWS, SUMACS)

This family consists of 83 genera with about 860 known species. Many members bear drupes, including economically important species such as cashew, mango, and pistachio. Some members produce the skin irritant urushiol, found in poison ivy, oak, and sumac.

SMOOTH SUMAC (AKA RED SUMAC, SHOEMAKE)
Rhus glabra and others

Edible parts/harvest time: Shoots in spring. Berries in late summer. Native.

The health benefits and dry storage properties of sumac berries make them a list-topper for foragers. High levels of antioxidants such as malic acid and vitamin C give them superfood status, and they have a delightful tart flavor!

Description: A colony-forming shrub to 15' tall, with leafy branches near the top of the stems. Bark is smooth and reddish brown on young plants, becoming grayish brown with raised horizontal lenticels. Alternate, compound leaves are odd-pinnate with 9–25 leaflets, forming on long, purplish stalks, with a whitish coating. Each leaflet is 4½" long to 1" wide, narrowly lanceolate, with shallow, toothed margins, a pale to dark green upper surface, and pale to white undersides. In late May–July, clusters of small white or pale green flowers form on erect panicles up to 10" long at the stem terminus. Female flowers mature August–September into tight, Christmas-tree-shaped clusters of small, red to dark maroon drupes. Stems and leaves exude a white latex when broken, and the leaves turn brilliant orange or red in fall.

Winged sumac (*R. copallinum*) is similar to smooth sumac but has a winged leaf rachis. Fragrant sumac (*R. aromatica*) differs from other *Rhus* species by having trifoliate leaves and small clusters of hairy red berries that form along the stem at leaf axils. Its leaves are quite aromatic and can be used for teas and flavoring.

Habitat/Range: Prefers open or disturbed habitats. Occurs in thickets, prairies, glades, old fields, woodland openings and their borders, fencerows, and along roadsides and railroads. Range is throughout the United States and Canada.

Fragrant sumac

Uses: Make awesome sumac lemonade by filling a gallon or quart jar about one-third full of fresh or dried berries, then cover with warm water. Steep overnight while periodically agitating the jar to release flavor. Strain through a cheesecloth or fine strainer to remove berries and stems, then sweeten to taste with your favorite sweetener. My favorite is a mix of agave nectar and stevia.

Tender shoots can be peeled and eaten raw or cooked; harvest when the inside is solid green, before the whitish pith forms. Berry clusters are best harvested as soon as they are ripe and before rain washes off the waxy, tart coating that contains the flavor. Once completely dried, they can be stored for long periods when tightly packed in lidded jars. The outer husks contain all the flavor; the small, hard seeds inside can be bitter. These flavorful husks can be used to make za'atar, a staple spice blend popular in Middle Eastern cuisine. The dried leaves are used in smoking mixtures. Pithy stems can be hollowed out for use as pipestems or blowtubes. All parts of the plant are used medicinally.

Warnings/Comments: Poison sumac (*Toxicondendron vernix*) has similar leaves and growth structure to edible *Rhus* species but has green to white berries along the main stem instead of red clustered berries. Its range is typically well east of the central grasslands. Once included in the genus *Rhus*, *Toxicondendron* species may produce contact dermatitis.

RECIPE

SUMAC MARGARITA

Pairs well with grilled prickly pear tacos and roasted ground cherry/tomato salsa.

¾ cup sumac lemonade, sweetened to taste

1½ ounces tequila

1 ounce triple sec or other orange liqueur

Optional: Flavor with wild fruit or berry syrups such as prickly pear fruit and chokecherry, and add crushed gooseberries or other wild berries or fruits.

Put ingredients in a shaker or large glass, shake or stir well, and serve over ice in a salt- or sugar-rimmed cocktail glass.

WILD SUMAC ZA'ATAR SPICE

2–3 tablespoons sumac berry powder

1 tablespoon ground cumin

1 teaspoon dried marjoram or oregano

1 tablespoon ground dried thyme

1 tablespoon ground toasted sesame seeds

1 teaspoon fine kosher salt

1 teaspoon freshly ground black pepper

Sumac berry powder: This will take a bit of time, as it needs to be done in small batches for best results. Making the powder requires a large amount of berry clusters. Air-dry them for a week or two, then remove berries from stems. The sumac powder by itself is very useful as a flavoring and can be used in jellies, as an ice cream or dessert topping, or wherever a tart flavor element is desired.

1. Place the berries in a food dehydrator (or large baking pan heated in a very low oven) until the husks are dry enough to crumble away from the inner seed when rubbed with your fingers.

2. Place in a food processor or blender in small batches to loosen the hulls. Be careful to not break up the seeds, as it may add a bitter flavor. If you don't have a food processor, this step can be done by placing a small amount in a wire strainer over a bowl and rubbing the broken husks, leaving the seeds in the strainer.

Za'atar spice: This isn't a set recipe; you can mix and match the spices listed, or add other spices or wild herbs for your own take on it. The combination makes an excellent meat rub or topping for roasted vegetables, soups, salads, sandwiches, and cooked dishes.

1. Combine the sumac berry powder with the other ingredients, shake well, and store in a sealed spice shaker or similar container.

APIACEAE (CARROTS, PARSLEY)

This large family has 3,700 species in 434 genera, including some of our most well-known domestic plants such as parsley, celery, coriander, cumin, dill, fennel, caraway, and parsnip. It also contains extremely toxic plants such as poison hemlock and water hemlock.

WILD CARROT (AKA QUEEN ANNE'S LACE)
Daucus carota and others

Edible parts/harvest time: Leaves whenever present and tender. Flowers in spring and summer. First-year roots in spring or fall. Seeds in fall through early winter. Introduced.

Toxic look-alikes: Poison hemlock, see "Warnings/Comments."

Description: This familiar biennial wildflower forms a basal rosette from a taproot during the first year, and produces a branching, flowering stalk up to 5' tall the second year. Fernlike alternate, compound leaves are up to 10" long, bipinnately divided into narrow segments, becoming shorter and sparser as they ascend the hairy stem. Blooms May–October. Flower heads are compound umbels forming at the stem terminus, generally round and flat-topped or domed, up to 5" across. They are densely packed with tiny, white, 5-petaled flowers, often with a small purple flower at the center. The flowers mature to small, elongated bristly seeds. The flower head usually becomes concave as it dries, and seeds fall into the bottom of the dried cup-shaped structure.

Habitat/Range: Found in open, disturbed habitats, pastures, old fields, tops of bluffs, glades, fencerows, roadsides, railroads, yards, gardens, and vacant lots. Native to Eurasia, naturalized across the United States and Canada. The smaller, native American wild carrot (*D. pusillus*) occurs in Oklahoma and Texas.

Uses: Use like domestic carrots. Young, first-year roots are good raw in salads or can be cooked in soups and other dishes. Second-year roots become tough and woody, but the fleshy outer part can be boiled in soups for flavor. Young, tender leaves and young flowers can be chopped and added raw to salads or other cooked greens. Flower heads can be fried in batter as fritters. Seeds are a good seasoning and are often present throughout the winter inside the dried flower heads. Do not consume unless identification is positive! The root should have a distinctive carrot smell.

Warnings/Comments: The extremely toxic poison hemlock has been misidentified as wild carrot, occasionally with fatal results (see the Poisonous Plants chapter for a full description). Second-year flowering plants are easily differentiated: Poison hemlock has smooth, purple-spotted hollow stems, chambered roots, and compound umbels that are more widely spaced than wild carrot. It also has larger, more robust leaves and does not smell like carrot. Identification can be more difficult while collecting when they are both emerging in early spring. If you've harvested carrot and then pull up hemlock, the carrot smell may remain on your hands and appear to be coming from the hemlock root, so don't take chances. Some sources advise to avoid all members of the family until characteristic differences are understood.

Poison hemlock vs. wild carrot with root

WESTERN BISCUITROOT (AKA CARROT-LEAF DESERT PARSLEY)
Lomatium foeniculaceum and others

Edible parts/harvest time: Greens in spring. Seeds in late spring and early summer. Roots in late summer after foliage starts to die back. Native, found most often in undisturbed or well-managed prairie habitat.

Description: This low-growing perennial is rarely over 18" tall, emerging from a slender to stubby, round, stout taproot. The plant has no flowering stem; the floral peduncle emerges directly from the ground with the leaf stalks, all of which are covered in white hairs. The greenish-gray leaves are up to 8" long, 2–3 times pinnately compound, and finely dissected, with leaf segments that are usually less than ¼" long. The main leaf stalks are stout, purplish, up to 12" long, with half of that length being the petiole. The tiny yellow, white, or occasionally purple 5-petaled flowers appear in April–June. They are arranged in tight compound umbels of up to 20 umbellets up to 4" across atop a peduncle that is 3–8" tall. The winged, oval fruits are ¼–½" long and split into a pair of 1-seeded segments, typical of others in the carrot family.

Habitat/Range: Occurs mostly in dry, open prairie hilltops and slopes, and prefers rocky limestone or chalk soils. Other species in the genus are found in a variety of prairie, desert, or montane habitats. Range is throughout the western half of the United States, from Texas to the Dakotas, east to Missouri.

Biscuitroot robust root SAMUEL THAYER

Uses: The edible taproot was a staple of plains-dwelling indigenous people: the root was dried and ground into flour to make large, flat "biscuits" referred to as konse. The root is covered by a brown skin that must be removed to expose the white, fibrous flesh, then it can be boiled, roasted, and used in soups and other cooked dishes. The young, tender leaves have a flavor like parsley. The first-year roots are best harvested in the dormancy of fall and winter, after the foliage has dried up. Harvesting wild roots is not recommended unless found in abundance, and only then with proper sustainable harvesting practices.

Warnings/Comments: Be certain of identification when consuming plants in the carrot family, however unlikely it would be to confuse this with toxic species. Cakes made from biscuitroot were mentioned in the Lewis and Clark journals as a trade item they obtained from the Shoshone. Over 85 species of *Lomatium* occur in the western United States. Many are edible or are used as medicine, while some have extremely limited ranges and are threatened.

PRAIRIE PARSLEY
Polytaenia nutallii and others

Edible parts/harvest time: Young shoots and top in spring. Flower clusters and seeds in mid- to late summer. Native, found mostly in prairie habitats.

For similar and toxic species, see "Warnings/Comments."

Description: A handsome biennial or shorter-lived perennial up to 3' tall emerging from a stout taproot, with yellow compound umbellate flowers. Foliage first emerges as a low basal rosette that may persist 2–4 years. Basal leaf blades are generally triangular, up to 6" long and 5" across, pinnate or bipinnate in structure, on pubescent petioles up to 4" long.

Individual leaflets are moderately to deeply divided into pinnate lobes, usually with a few coarse teeth at the margins. The stout, mostly pubescent flowering stalk is vertically ribbed, pale green to brownish red in color, usually unbranched except toward the apex. Alternate stem leaves resemble basal leaves but are widely separated, becoming less divided and smaller as they ascend the stem. The central stalk terminates in flat to dome-shaped compound umbellate flower heads up to 3–4" across; occasionally a few smaller lateral umbels will develop on long peduncles from the upper leaf axils. Umbels consist of 10–20 smaller umbellets, each about 1" across with 10–15 flowers about ⅛" across. Individual flowers have 5 yellow petals surrounded by 5 green sepals, folded inward. Each flower is replaced by a dry fruit resembling a dill seed, becoming ¼" or longer at maturity. Immature fruits are green, maturing to yellow and eventually brown. Each fruit consists of a pair of seeds that later develop winged margins to aid in wind distribution. Texas prairie parsley (*P. texana*) is similar with similar uses, but its range is limited to central and eastern Texas and southern Oklahoma. These two species are the only representatives of the genus.

Habitat/Range: Occurs in upland prairies, savannas, fields and borders, limestone and chert glades, thinly wooded bluffs, ditches, and along roadsides. Prefers dry, rocky soils. Prairie parsley is an indicator plant of original prairie. Range is the eastern third of Texas, Oklahoma, Kansas, and southeast Nebraska, and to the east from Louisiana north to Wisconsin. It is listed as threatened in several eastern states at the limits of its range.

Uses: Young shoots and leaves can be boiled as a potherb or added to cooked dishes. Flower heads can be eaten raw in salads or deep-fried in tempura batter as fritters. Seeds can be used as a seasoning akin to dill seeds. The root is edible but not palatable. Tea from the seeds has been used to treat diarrhea. It is a handsome prairie wildflower that would benefit from being planted in flower gardens and otherwise encouraged in appropriate habitats to supplement wild populations.

Golden Alexanders

Warnings/Comments: As with all carrot relatives, take care with identification before consuming. There are other related species with similar yellow flower clusters: Golden Alexander (*Zizia aurea*) has similar uses to prairie parsley; its shiny compound leaves are odd-pinnate with 3 or 5 leaflets that have finely serrated margins. Its fruits are ribbed but not winged, and the central flower in an umbellet is usually stalkless. Meadow parsnip (*Thaspium* spp.) has broader, trifoliate leaves and is not considered edible. Wild parsnip (*Pastinaca sativa*) is a much larger plant up to 5' tall with a larger flower cluster up to 8" across, duller, somewhat greenish-yellow flowers, and once-compound leaves with up to 15 leaflets. The introduced invasive wild parsnip has edible roots, but its sap contains toxic furanocoumarins, which can make skin sensitive to ultraviolet radiation. Skin exposure to the sap combined with sunlight can cause severe burns and blisters within 24–48 hours.

APOCYNACEAE (MILKWEEDS)

A family of 415 genera and about 4,600 species of trees, shrubs, woody vines, and herbs, found mostly in tropical and subtropical areas of the world. Members of the family have milky, often toxic juice, smooth-margined leaves, and flowers in clusters. Our native milkweeds are in the subfamily Asclepiadoideae; most have showy flowers and seedpods that split to release tufted seeds.

COMMON MILKWEED
Asclepias syriaca and others

Edible parts/harvest time: Shoots and leaves in spring. Flowers and buds May–August. Seedpods July–September. Native, common.

Description: An erect perennial up to 6', with a single, stout stem that branches near the top when flower clusters form. Opposite, petioled leaves are up to 7" long, broadly elliptical, with a prominent central vein and smooth margins. Fragrant blooms appear in May–August; umbellate flower clusters up to 4½" across form on pedicels at leaf axils and at the stem terminus. Individual flowers are ¼" across, light pink to pale purple, each with 5 recurved petals and 5 erect, curved hoods. Teardrop-shaped seedpods grow to 4" long, covered with soft, slender projections. All parts exude a white, milky latex when torn.

Habitat/Range: Found in mostly open habitats, in prairies, pastures, roadsides, fencerows, woodland borders, old fields, and disturbed waste areas. Occurs over most of the central and eastern United States and in Canada.

Uses: Fresh flowers have a wonderful floral scent and are excellent when raw, sprinkled over fish, salads, soups, or desserts. Young, tender shoots, leaves, flower buds, and small seedpods are good after steaming or boiling; some compare the flavor to okra without the slime. Young, tender pods can be boiled, cleaned out, and filled with various stuffings. Older references say the latex sap is bitter until cooked, but the topmost paired leaves on younger plants are quite tasty raw as a trail nibble. The fibrous, outer skin of the stem makes good cordage. The dry seed fluff is good clothing insulation or fire-starter, and the latex is said to be good for removing warts.

Milkweed shoot at collection stage

Pod at collection stage

Warnings/Comments: Many narrow-leaved milkweed species are too toxic to consume. Other edible broad-leaved species are showy milkweed (*A. speciosa*) and purple milkweed. (*A. purpurea*). Do not consume if any bitterness persists after cooking. Native milkweeds are a critical host plant of monarch butterflies; please harvest responsibly and only when found in abundance.

STUFFED MILKWEED PODS

15–20 milkweed pods, harvested young before they become tough

4 ounces cream cheese, softened

2 tablespoons finely chopped onion

2 garlic cloves, finely chopped

2 tablespoons finely chopped wild or store-bought mushrooms

1 small jalapeño, finely chopped (or substitute 2 tablespoons diced green chilies)

2 slices cooked bacon, chopped (optional)

1 teaspoon salt

1 teaspoon black pepper

Grated cheese of your choice

Optional: Use wild seasoning herbs such as prairie parsley, horseweed, wild bergamot, etc. or your favorite spices and seasonings to taste

1. Bring milkweed pods to a boil in a large pot of water for 10 minutes. Drain, let cool, and set aside.

2. Place the softened cream cheese and the rest of the ingredients (except grated cheese) in a bowl, blend well, and set aside.

3. Slice the pods open with a paring knife and remove the seeds and silk. Spoon in cream cheese filling until the pod is full. Place on a parchment paper–lined baking sheet.

4. Sprinkle grated cheese over the filled pods, place in oven, and bake 15–20 minutes at 375°F. If desired, broil to crisp up the cheese. Serve warm.

MILKWEED FLOWER CORDIAL

2–3 cups milkweed flowers, cleaned and destemmed

8 cups water

2½ cups organic cane, maple, or white sugar

2 tablespoons white vinegar

2 lemons, sliced in thin strips

Mason jars

1. Prep flowers by cutting away stem parts (scissors come in handy).

2. Pour water and sugar into a large bowl, mix to dissolve sugar, then add vinegar.

3. Evenly divide the flowers and sliced lemons into 2 (or more) mason jars, then add the water mixture. Mark and date the containers, cover with cheesecloth and rubber bands, or keep the lid loose for gasses to escape. Let sit 4 days at room temperature; sunlight may help release flavor. Stir once daily or tighten the lid to shake, just be sure to loosen the lid again after shaking.

4. On the fourth day, use gloves to crush the flowers to release flavors, then remove and strain out remaining flowers and lemons. For an uncarbonated cordial syrup, use more sugar and a bit of citric acid, then refrigerate after straining. For a carbonated cordial, seal jars for a day or two after straining to build up carbonation; burp once or more daily if sealed more than a day. Keep inside a lidded bucket during carbonation in the unlikely event of an explosion if gasses build up too much pressure.

5. After straining, place in serving bottles or jars, refrigerate, and enjoy!

ASTERACEAE (ASTERS, SUNFLOWERS, COMPOSITE-FLOWERED PLANTS)

This family includes over 32,000 species in over 1,900 genera, rivaled only by Orchidaceae in number of species. It contains many economically and horticulturally important species such as lettuce, artichokes, and sunflowers, and may represent up to 10 percent of all native flora in any given region.

RAGWEEDS
Ambrosia trífida and others

Edible parts/harvest time: Shoots and leaves in late spring and early summer. Flowers and seeds in late summer to fall. Native and common, often an aggressive colonizer.

Ragweeds are an unwelcome sight to many, as they are prodigious producers of the wind-borne pollen responsible for hay fever and many summer allergies. Seeds of various ragweed species were prehistorically cultivated for their high protein and oil content. The crushed leaves of all species exude a somewhat strong odor.

Description: Tall ragweed is a weedy annual up to 12' tall, with green stems covered in white hairs. Opposite leaves have finely serrated margins, are up to 12" long and 8" across, usually palmately divided into 3–5 lobes. Lower, larger leaves are on long petioles and have a rough outer surface. Smaller leaves nearer the inflorescence become lanceolate and hairy. Most upper stems terminate in a 3–6"-long cylindrical spike of flowers, with 1 or more smaller spikes near its base. Blooms in mid- to late summer, with small yellowish-green

Tall ragweed seeds

flowers that have no petals or sepals. They are densely arranged around each spike, occurring in small drooping clusters less than ¼" across. Seeds are achenes up to ⅛" long, dark brown, and obovoid or conical in shape, clustered below the flowers. Each seed has a short beak at its apex and about 4 tiny tubercles around the edge of its upper margin, appearing crown-like. Common ragweed (*A. artemisiifolia*) is up to 3' tall, with ornate, 2–3 times pinnately lobed hairy leaves that can be alternate or opposite. Western ragweed (*A. psilostachia*) is similar to common ragweed but has generally paler leaves that are single pinnately lobed, and it has a more western range. Flower structure and seed shape is similar in all ragweeds.

Tall ragweed with shoot

Western ragweed

Habitat/Range: Often forms large colonies in open or disturbed ground in prairies, pastures, old fields, cropland, ditches, banks of streams, ponds, and marshes, open woodland areas and their borders, and along roadsides, railroads, and fencerows. Both giant and common ragweed are found from New Mexico to Montana east to the coastal states. Western ragweed occurs from east Texas to Minnesota, west to southern California and Arizona, and north to eastern Montana, with scattered isolated populations in the upper Mountain West.

Uses: Despite its bad reputation, ragweed shouldn't be overlooked. Its flowers and seeds are a nutritional powerhouse, with a wheat bran–like flavor and a content of 47 percent protein and 28 percent fat. Roasted, ground seeds and flowers are good as an additive to flours, wild seedcakes, soups, and cooked dishes, and can be mixed with other wild seeds for flavor when lacto-fermenting or pickling food. Seeds should be collected early before they become hard and tough. Young shoots and tender leaves can have a somewhat strong odor and flavor; this can be reduced by soaking overnight in cold water, boiling in 1 or 2 waters, and/or mixing them with milder greens. They were also boiled to harvest the seed oil.

Warnings/Comments: Those with severe ragweed allergies may want to avoid this plant. Folk remedies suggest that regularly eating small amounts of the leaves mixed with other foods from the time it emerges till pollen season will help reduce allergic reactions. Ragweeds are an agricultural pest in many regions and may be developing herbicide-resistant strains. On the positive side, they are also being used in phytoremediation to remove lead, cobalt, zinc, and other heavy metals from contaminated areas. Collections of ragweed seeds are commonly found in prehistoric archaeological sites; they were selectively cultivated to produce seeds larger than found in common varieties. The plant has had extensive uses medicinally, which may help explain the genus name *Ambrosia* (food of the gods or a reference to immortality).

RECIPE

AMBROSIA FLATBREAD

1½ cups ripe ragweed seeds, or a mix of curly dock, lamb's quarter, amaranth, mallow, or any other wild seeds, roasted and crushed or ground

¾ cup white unbleached flour

½ teaspoon wild bergamot and/or lemon beebalm leaves, dried and ground (or substitute oregano)

1 teaspoon salt or to taste

1 cup water

1 teaspoon honey or sweetener of choice

1. Combine dry ingredients in a bowl.

2. Add a small amount of water a small bit at a time, mixing dry ingredients into a dough.

3. Mix in honey. The dough should hold together in a clump. If too wet, add more flour.

4. Place dough ball on a floured cutting board or flat surface. Roll or press into a thin cracker-like layer and cut into desired shapes/sizes. Transfer to a greased baking sheet.

5. Bake at 375°F or until crisp, taking care not to burn.

6. Let cool. Serve with wild pesto or dip/condiment of your choice.

COMMON BURDOCK (AKA LESSER BURDOCK)
Arctium minus and others

Edible parts/harvest time: Shoots and leaf petioles in late spring and early summer. Roots anytime, but best in fall after the top dies. Introduced, common.

Description: A large-leaved biennial that forms a first-year basal rosette from a taproot; branched flowering stems emerge the second year. Basal leaves are ovate to broadly cordate, up to 2' long and 1½' across, with a dull green upper surface, wavy margins, and pale, woolly undersides. Petioles are long and hollow, usually furrowed along the top surface. Flowering stems are often hollow and up to 6' tall, ridged and hairy, later becoming smooth and with prominent longitudinal veins. Leaves on flowering stems are alternate, usually smaller than basal leaves. Flowers appear in June–October, clustered on racemes at the stem terminus or at the leaf axil. Each flower is a globe-shaped involucre covered in bracts that terminate in hooked spines, ¾–1" across, with tubular, pale lavender or purple corollas and white, elongated styles. These flower heads dry out to become burs that catch on passing animals or humans for seed distribution. Great burdock (*A. lappa*) and woolly burdock (*A. tomentosum*) are two other introduced burdocks found in the United States but are less common.

Habitat/Range: Common in barnyards, pastures, old fields, thickets, fencerows, woodland and cropland borders, power line cuts, and roadsides. Prefers disturbed, open ground but can colonize paths and animal trails in woodlands. Native to Eurasia, naturalized throughout the United States and Canada.

A good-sized burdock root

Uses: Young, first-year roots can be eaten raw, slow-roasted, boiled, or fried like potatoes. Older first-year roots can be peeled of their bitter exterior and boiled or added to soups. Young shoots of flower stems can be peeled and cooked as a vegetable, lacto-fermented, or pickled; pre-flowering older stems can be parboiled, then peeled and cooked if they aren't too tough. Petioles of basal rosette leaves can be cooked as a vegetable. The root was combined with dandelion leaves and other ingredients to make beer. The root is also known for its immune-building, antioxidant, and aphrodisiac properties. Studies on burdock seeds show effectiveness for treating tumors and other cancers.

Warnings/Comments: Cultivars with larger, fleshier roots (sold as gobo root) are grown and sold commercially for culinary use; they can be found in most Asian markets in the United States. In 1941, the Swiss inventor George de Mestral noticed the hooked spines of burdock seeds embedded in his dog's fur and used the idea to invent a fastener he later patented as Velcro.

RECIPE

SOUTHERN-FRIED BURDOCK SHOOTS

Select only tender shoots; tough shoots will be harder to cut. Harvest by cutting close to the ground, then trim the leaf stalks. The inside of the stalk should be solid; if a hole appears in the center, it may be too tough. Peel by using a paring knife to grab and strip off the tough skin; slice away any remaining parts that appear to have grooves.

2–3 young burdock shoots, peeled and sliced into ¾-inch pieces

1 egg, beaten

1 cup (or more) 50-50 mix of cornstarch and unbleached flour

1 tablespoon olive oil

Salt and pepper to taste

1. Boil shoots in salted water for 3–5 minutes; remove. A bit of lemon juice will keep them from oxidizing and turning brown.
2. Put shoots in a bowl with the beaten egg, then remove and roll them in the flour mixture.
3. Place in a skillet with the hot oil and fry until brown.

RECIPE

KINPIRA GOBO (ASIAN STIR-FRIED BURDOCK ROOT)

2 pounds peeled burdock root, sliced thin diagonally (cover with water until ready to cook)

2 tablespoons vegetable oil

¼ pound carrots, peeled and cut into short, thin strips

1½ teaspoons mirin (sweet rice wine)

1 tablespoon sugar

½ tablespoon sake

1 tablespoon soy sauce

1 teaspoon sesame seeds

1. Put the burdock roots into a skillet with the hot oil. Cook for a couple minutes and stir in the carrots.
2. Add the mirin, sugar, and sake; cook until the liquid is gone.
3. Mix in the soy sauce and cook till tender. Serve topped with sesame seeds.

SPANISH NEEDLES
(AKA DEVIL'S PITCHFORKS, BEGGARTICKS)
Bidens bipinnata and others

Spanish needles with seeds

Edible parts/harvest time: Shoots, young leaves in early to late summer. Native, common.
Description: Several species can be found in the central grasslands; all are annuals with disk florets and long and slender or oval and flat achenes with 2–4 barbed awns. Some have either white or yellow petaloid ray flowers; some are without rays. All are roughly 1–3' tall, branching occasionally in the upper half of the stem. Species found commonly in the central grasslands region are *B. frondosa*, *B. tripartita*, *B. aristosa*, *B. bipinnata*, and several others; all have edible leaves and similar common names.

Spanish needles (*B. bipinnata*) leaves have a fernlike appearance. The leaf blades are double or triple pinnate, medium green, and mostly hairless, up to 8" long and 4" across, on 2"-long petioles. The segments of the blades are ovate, lanceolate, or oblanceolate with wedged bottoms and blunt tips; segment margins are irregularly dentate. The upper stems terminate in individual flower heads on long peduncles. Each flower head is about ½" long and ¼" across with numerous disk florets in the center and 0–5 ray florets along its upper margin. The disk floret corollas are yellow and tubular. The yellow ray florets are about ⅛"

Bearded beggarticks

long and oval to oblong in shape. Each flower head is replaced by a globoid seedhead about 1" across. The long, slender achenes spread outward from the center in all directions; individual mature seeds are dark brown and 4-angled, with 2–4 short, barbed awns at the tip.

Devil's beggarticks (*B. frondosa*) has opposite compound leaves on long petioles that are usually odd-pinnate with 3 or 5 leaflets; simple alternate leaves will occasionally form near the flower heads. Individual leaflets are up to 3" long and 1" across, lanceolate, broadly serrated, with long, pointed tips. A few upper stems terminate in individual flower heads about ¾–1" across on long stalks; some stalks may have 1–2 additional flower heads. Blooms in late summer to early fall, with flower heads consisting of numerous disk florets with yellow corollas and no petaloid rays. The florets mature to produce flattened dark achenes that terminate in a pair of long, slender barbed awns. The leaves often turn dark purple in fall. Bearded beggarticks (*B. aristosa*) has similar foliage to *B. frondosa* but has large, showy yellow flowers.

Habitat/Range: Occurs in moist black-soil prairies, damp meadows, thickets, marshy seeps, pastures, croplands, abandoned fields, and along borders of streams, ponds, or lakes, railroads, and roadsides. Prefers disturbed ground. Numerous Bidens species can be found throughout the United States, although some are more restricted in range.

Uses: For a plant that turns up nearly everywhere, species in the genus *Bidens* have been mostly overlooked in foraging resources. Shoots, tops, and young leaves are boiled as a mild potherb. Leaves of some species are used raw in salads. A nibble and spit test is handy to determine flavor; they are typically mild. Flowers of some species can be used in salads and to make wine. Dried leaves are used as tea or in smoking mixtures.

Warnings/Comments: Avoid spreading seeds into new areas, as some species can be aggressive pests. Members of the genus are widespread in many habitats and edible, and some are magnets for important pollinators. All plant parts have been used medicinally to treat various ailments. They are despised as an annoying weed because of the barbed seeds that cling to clothing and pet fur. Not to be confused with beggar's lice, which is a common name describing a triangular-seeded species in the genus *Desmondium*, in the Pea family.

TALL THISTLE (AKA MEADOW OR ROADSIDE THISTLE)
Cirsium altissimum and others

Edible parts/harvest time: Shoots, young leaves, peeled stems and roots in late spring and summer. Seeds in fall. Native and introduced.

I learned about this plant from a Cherokee elder in Georgia during his rivercane blowgun class. A dart was made from a sliver of cane, and thistle seedhead fluff was spun onto the end of the dart with string for fletching. The bonus was learning that the peeled young thistle stems were delicious!

Description: A biennial or perennial with spiny leaves, erect stems to 8', and showy, purplish-pink flowers. First-year plants form a basal rosette; flower stalks emerge the second year. Main stems and branches are sparsely hairy, sometimes pubescent, with longitudinal ridges. Alternate leaves are up to 8" long and 3" across, generally lanceolate to elliptic, with white woolly undersides and sparse hairs on the upper surface. Similar introduced species like bull thistle do not have leaves with white undersides. Leaves become smaller as they ascend the stem. Margins are usually dentate to lobed and spiny, occasionally smooth with prickles. Numerous blooms appear in July–October, forming singly at the ends of upper branches. Flowers are up to 2" across, with multitudes of disk florets in a bulb-shaped head, each with 5 pink, tubular corollas. The flowers dry into brown seedheads, opening to expose a fluffy bundle of numerous white pappus bristles attached to small, bullet-shaped seeds for wind distribution.

Field thistle (*C. discolor*) is a similar native that can interbreed with tall thistle. Wavy-leaved thistle (*C. undulatum*) ranges from the midwestern prairie states throughout the Mountain West. It has very wavy and spiny leaf margins and is typically paler in color than others in the genus.

Habitat/Range: Found commonly along roadsides and in pastures, power line cuts, prairies, glades, old fields, streambanks, bases of bluffs, open bottomlands, and upland forest openings and borders. Range is eastern and midwestern United States, west to North Dakota and Texas. Absent from New England.

Peeled stem of bull thistle

Uses: Young, tender shoots of some species can be cooked as a potherb; others may need the larger spines trimmed. Cut larger stems off at the ground when they are under waist-high and peel off the tough outer skin to expose the crunchy center. The center white core is somewhat sweet and can be eaten raw as a trail nibble, cooked, or added to other dishes and wild lacto-ferments. Roots of young basal rosettes can be eaten raw, roasted, or cooked; if present in larger specimens, remove the tough outer rind and toss them into soups. The center section and midrib of the large basal rosette leaves are a delicious treat in the field. Cut the leaf at the base, hold it by the midrib, and use a sharp knife to slice the leaf blades off each side to remove the spines. Seeds can be roasted and ground for an additive to flour or seedcakes. All parts of the plant have been used medicinally.

Warnings/Comments: The introduced bull thistle (*C. vulgare*) and musk thistle (*Carduus nutans*) are noxious weeds in many areas, so best to avoid spreading seeds. All true thistles are edible.

HORSEWEED (AKA MARE'S TAIL)
Conyza canadensis

Edible parts/harvest time: Shoots, leaves in late spring to summer. Flower buds in mid- to late summer. Native.

Description: A stout-stemmed annual with a single, hairy stem and densely arranged alternate leaves occurring along the length of the stem, giving it a whorled and weedy appearance. On large specimens, the stem may branch profusely in the uppermost part during flowering. Individual leaves are elliptic or narrowly lanceolate, 2–3½" long and ¼–½" across, growing smaller as they ascend the stem. Lower, larger leaves may have sparsely dentate margins, upper stem leaves are typically smaller with smooth margins, and both have conspicuous hairs along their edges. Blooms June–November, with numerous small flowers forming on a large panicle at the stem terminus, often with smaller panicles emerging at the upper leaf axils. The panicle stems develop leaflike bracts up to 1" long. Individual flowers are about ¼" long, urn-shaped, with tiny, inconspicuous petaloid rays.

Habitat/Range: Found in prairies, glades, pastures, vacant lots, fencerows, gardens, openings in woodlands, and along roadsides and streambanks. Prefers open, disturbed ground. Range is throughout the United States and southern provinces of Canada.

Uses: Young, tender leaves have a strong herblike flavor with a spicy, almost hot after-taste. They are great when sparingly added to salads or other cooked dishes for flavor. They can be ground into a seasoning that some-what resembles tarragon. Young shoots and leaves can be boiled as a potherb. Flower buds and tender tops can be pulverized and added to cooked dishes. The dried stem is one of the best materials for a friction fire hand-drill spindle.

Warnings/Comments: Horseweed is a seri-ous agricultural pest, especially in corn and soybean fields. It was one of the first plants to develop a resistance to glyphosate, first recorded in 2001 in Delaware. The genus con-tains around 167 accepted species, with several similar to horseweed.

SUNROOT (AKA SUNCHOKE, JERUSALEM ARTICHOKE)
Helianthus tuberosus and other sunflowers

Edible parts/harvest time: Shoots, leaves, and buds in spring to midsummer. Tubers in late summer but best after the first frost in fall and winter. Seeds in late summer and fall. Native.

Spoiler: This sunflower is neither an artichoke nor from Jerusalem. Years ago, my assistant included the raw starchy tubers of a newly discovered patch of sunroot in every meal dur-ing a wilderness skills class. The high inulin content fueled epic gas production, and that night we reenacted the campfire scene in the film *Blazing Saddles*! They are called "Farti-chokes" for good reason.

Description: A perennial with a hairy, green to reddish-brown stem up to 12' tall, usually with multiple branches on the top half, and flower heads on long peduncles at the stem terminus. Leaves are on ¼–2" winged petioles, opposite, becoming alternate as they ascend the stem. Leaf blades are up to 7" long and 4" across, lance shaped to broadly ovate-acute, pubescent to hairy, with entire to broadly toothed margins. Flower heads are typical of sunflowers, consisting of a central cluster of disk florets surrounded by 10–20 yellow ray florets to 3½" across. Tubers are irregular, round to elongated, up to 4" long and 2" across,

occasionally spreading to form large colonies. Maximilian sunflower (*H. maximilianii*) also has edible tubers and seeds; it is a tall, erect perennial with slender, hairy stems up to 10' tall. The stem is mostly unbranched except where the flower heads emerge at the top. Alternate, sessile leaves are lanceolate, up to 12" long and 2" wide, folded along the midrib, and are curved downward. Leaf margins are smooth or with widely spaced shallow serrations. Flowers are typical yellow sunflowers, about 4" across. There are several *Helianthus* species of sunflower found in the central grasslands, all with edible seeds and flower heads.

Habitat/Range: Sunroot occurs in openings in rich upland and bottomland forests, woodland borders, pastures, roadsides, fencerows, streambanks, pond edges, disturbed, ground, and moist depressions in upland prairies. Range is throughout the United States and Canada, absent in the Desert Southwest and western Canadian provinces.

Uses: The tubers are mildly sweet, nutty, and crunchy when eaten raw (see Warnings/Comments) and are a great addition to salads and other raw vegetable dishes. Can be cooked like potatoes: boiled, roasted, fried, or added to soups. They are also good for pickling or lacto-fermenting. Best when harvested late, between the first frost and early spring, when the indigestible polysaccharides have converted to digestible sugars. **Note:** Soaking/cooking the tubers in lemon juice or pickling will help de-gasify them. The flower buds, flowers, and young leaves can be shredded into salads or folded into mashed potatoes or other cooked dishes for a peppery element. The young flower stem shoots can be eaten raw or cooked as a vegetable. As in all sunflowers, the seeds are edible but are much smaller than the domesticated varieties. They are usually eaten shell and all.

Maximilian sunflower with plains sunflower (inset)

Warnings/Comments: Overconsumption of raw tubers can occasionally cause stomach distress, but usually the side effect is extreme flatulence (post-meal entertainment for those so inclined). The species is widely cultivated and sold commercially as sunchokes. A variety of commercial bioproducts are derived from the tubers, including inulin, fructose, natural fungicides, bioethanol, and antioxidants used as food additives. The tubers are also distilled into several types of alcoholic spirits and marketed in Europe as Topi and Rossler.

Smash-fried sunroots and wild salad

SMASH-FRIED SUNROOTS IN PANKO AND LEMON/WILD HERB BUTTER

6 cleaned sunroot tubers with dark spots cut out (use more or less depending on size of tubers, or substitute Maximilian sunflower tubers)

1 lemon, squeezed, with a bit of skin, zested

2+ tablespoons unsalted butter

1 tablespoon finely minced wild onion/garlic bulb, or dash of garlic powder

¼ cup or so of freshly picked, finely chopped wild seasoning herb leaves such as pineapple weed, horseweed, wild bergamot, fragrant sumac, wild onion, wild carrot, etc. Or substitute a dash of thyme, oregano, or seasoning herb of your choice.

1 cup unseasoned panko

1½ tablespoons good-quality cooking oil (Wildwoods Orchards Hickory Oil)

Sea salt

1. In a medium saucepan, add sunroots to 1 inch of salted water and half the lemon juice and bring to a boil, then reduce heat to maintain a simmer. Cook about 10–15 minutes until tender to where a knife meets little resistance; don't overcook to where they are mushy. Drain sunroots in a fine-mesh strainer or colander and allow to cool.

2. Place one at a time on a cutting board and use the bottom of a heavy skillet to press firmly on each sunroot until it is flattened but still in one piece. Don't press so hard that they break apart.

3. Melt butter in a small bowl with remaining lemon juice, zest, onion/garlic, and chopped wild herb leaves.

4. Pour panko into a plate. Gently press both sides of each sunroot patty into it to embed the crumbs. Set patties aside on a paper towel.

5. In a large cast-iron skillet, heat oil to shimmering. Add sunroot patties in a single layer with a bit of space in between and cook without moving for about 3 minutes or until browned. Add about three-quarters of the lemon/herb butter to the pan and allow to melt, then carefully flip the patties. Spoon the remaining butter over them and cook for about 5–8 minutes or until browned on the second side.

6. Transfer sunroots to a serving plate. Garnish with a wild herbs or other fresh wild green leaves or flowers and sprinkle with flaky salt. Serve while warm.

7. Optional: Top with a mushroom/wine sauce. Start with a traditional flour roux, add garlic powder, butter-sautéed wild or domestic mushrooms, and a splash of marsala or other wine. Slowly add milk or cream and simmer to thicken. Salt or season to taste.

MARSH ELDER (AKA SUMPWEED)
Iva annua

Edible parts/harvest time: Seeds in late summer to fall. Native.

Description: A weedy herbaceous annual 1–5' tall with broad leaves and spikelike flowers. The central stem is branched, light green to reddish green, and usually hairy toward the top. Opposite leaves occur along the lower stems; some upper-most leaves may be alternate. Lower leaves are on pale green and relatively hairy petioles up to 2½" long. Leaf blades are 1–6" long and ½–4" across, lanceolate, ovate or deltate, with sharply pointed tips. The leaves get smaller as they ascend the stem. Leaf margins are coarsely serrate; some uppermost leaves may be tooth-less. Each leaf usually has one central and two lateral veins that are prominent and mostly parallel. The upper stems resemble ragweed flower heads, terminating in narrow racemes of flower heads, about 2–8" long and less than ¼" across, on short hairy pedun-cles. Additional racemes are often produced from the axils of the upper leaves. Small, indi-vidual flowers have 8–15 central staminate florets and 3–5 peripheral pistillate florets with greenish-white to greenish-yellow corollas. Each flower is surrounded by 4–5 floral bracts joined at the base, forming a nodding cup-like shape. These floral bracts are initially green, later becoming red or brown with hairy exteriors. The crushed foliage of the plant emits a camphor-like odor.

Habitat/Range: Occurs in moist prairies, low margins of rivers and ponds, prairie swales and sloughs, ditches, cropland, fallow fields, waste areas, and roadside ditches. Prefers moist open, disturbed ground. Range is Texas to Nebraska east to the Atlantic coastal states.

Uses: Seeds can be roasted or parched, then ground and added to other seeds such as dock, lamb's quarter, and climbing buckwheat. Seeds can also be simmered in water to extract the oil, which rises to the top where it can be ladled off.

Warnings/Comments: Along with its relative ragweed, marsh elder was cultivated for its edible seeds by Native Americans around 4,000 years ago in today's central and eastern United States as part of the Eastern Agricultural Complex. It was especially important to indigenous peoples, including the Hopewell culture in present-day Missouri and Illinois. The edible parts contain 32 percent protein and 45 percent oil. Like ragweed, marsh elder can be a severe potential allergen, and it has a strong odor that is disagreeable to some. It was probably abandoned as a crop when maize became available. The larger cultivated variety (*Iva annua macrocarpa*) disappeared long before the arrival of the first Europeans.

OXEYE DAISY (AKA COMMON DAISY)
Leucanthemum vulgare

Edible parts/harvest time: Shoots, leaves, flowers and buds, roots in late spring through summer. Large basal rosette leaves appear in spring and/or late fall. Introduced.

Description: An herbaceous showy perennial up to 3' tall. The mostly unbranched, leaved stem emerges from a basal rosette. Basal and middle leaves are on petioles, 2–6" long, dark green, ovate to spoon shaped, with coarsely dentate or lobed margins. Alternate leaves on the stem are lanceolate and sessile, with sparse, bluntly serrated margins, becoming smaller as they ascend the stem. Blooms May–August. Flowers appear singly at the stem terminus, each with a yellow central disk and 20–30 radial, white ray florets, up to 2" across.

Basal leaves at collection stage

Habitat/Range: Found primarily in open or disturbed ground, in pastures, fields, glades, prairies, roadsides, lawns, and open-canopy woodlands. Native to Europe and temperate Asia, naturalized throughout North America.

Uses: Raw, tender leaves, unopened buds, and young flowers have great flavor as a trail nibble, in salads, or as a pizza topping. They add a nice flavor to any dish. The large basal rosettes are best when available in late fall/early winter and spring; leaves on flowering stems can be used anytime. Flower buds can be marinated, added to lacto-ferments, or pickled and used as capers. Fresh or dried flowers make a nice herbal tea. Young roots can be eaten raw or cooked. The plant has been used medicinally for centuries and is said to have a calming effect like chamomile.

Warnings/Comments: Listed as a noxious weed in some states due to its aggressive colonizing nature. Allergies and contact dermatitis have been reported from this plant but are extremely rare. Several cultivars and hybrids such as Shasta daisy are commercially available for flower gardens.

PINEAPPLE WEED (AKA WILD CHAMOMILE)
Matricaria discoidea and others

WALTER SIEGMUND, WIKIMEDIA COMMONS

Edible parts/harvest time: Leaves and flowers whenever present. Introduced.

Description: A small, bushy-appearing annual, 3–10" tall with smooth stems emerging from a branching taproot, delicate fernlike leaves, and small greenish-yellow rayless flower heads. Alternate leaves are up to 3" long and ¾" across, divided into slender, linear lobes that may be simple, double, or triple pinnately compound. Blooms May–October, with flower heads forming on ½–1" stalks from the upper leaf axils. Individual cone- or globe-shaped flower heads are about ¼–½" across, consisting of numerous greenish-yellow disk florets without ray florets and several overlapping green bracts at the base. Each disk floret is replaced by an oblong achene. The entire plant exudes a sweet pineapple-like odor when crushed.

Habitat/Range: Occurs in barnyards, rocky pastures, waste areas, edges of driveways and footpaths, and gravelly areas along railroads and roadways. It is most common near areas of human habitation and rarely found in pristine habitats. Pineapple weed prefers open, disturbed areas and tolerates poor habitats in compacted soils that are clay, gravelly, or sandy. Range is thought to have originally been Asia and the US Pacific Northwest. It has naturalized in most states but is absent in the Southeast.

Uses: Young leaves and flower heads are a great addition to green salads, best collected before the flower heads bloom. They can also be added to cooked dishes for flavor. The green or dried leaves make an excellent medicinal tea used to treat various ailments such as diarrhea and stomach pains. The crushed leaves were used by some indigenous tribes as a perfume and insect repellent.

Warnings/Comments: Some may be allergic to this plant. Before flowering, young pineapple weed may slightly resemble stinking chamomile (*Anthemis cotula*) or toxic dog fennel (*Eupatorium capillifolium*); both are introduced plants in southeastern states. A smell test will help differentiate, as both these plants have foliage with an unpleasant odor when crushed. The introduced, cultivated German chamomile (*Matricaria chamomilla*) has similar foliage and uses but is generally taller with flowers that have white ray florets surrounding the central disk.

SOCHAN (AKA CUT-LEAVED CONEFLOWER, GREEN-HEADED CONEFLOWER)
Rudbeckia laciniata

Leaf at collection stage

Edible parts/harvest time: Shoots and leaves in spring to midsummer. Basal leaves appear again in fall. Native.

Description: An herbaceous perennial 3–9' tall, sometimes forming large colonies from spreading rhizomes. Large basal leaves are up to 12" long and 10" across, alternate, deeply lobed in 3–7 segments, sometimes pinnate with a pair of basal leaflets and a lobed terminal leaflet, becoming smaller and with fewer lobes as they ascend the branching stems. Upper leaves are lanceolate, lacking lobes, often on winged petioles. Blooms July–September. Flowers are 2–3" across, composite, with 6–12 drooping, yellow petals and a dome-shaped center disc. They form singly or on cyme-like clusters of 2"-long stalks at the stem apex and tips of branches.

Habitat/Range: Found in moist soil conditions in floodplains, bottomland forests, streambanks, partially shaded sloughs, wet fields, ditches, seeps, and forest edges. Widespread over most of the United States and Canada, absent from Oregon, Nevada, and California.

Uses: This plant has a nice herb/celery flavor. Young, tender raw leaves are a great salad addition. Leaves and shoots are used as a potherb, collected when they first come up in the spring. Older, larger leaves can be cut up for boiled greens until they get too strong or too tough to eat. Tender stems tops can be peeled and cooked as a vegetable. Check locations in late fall, after the flowering stem dies back, to harvest the tender basal leaves that pop up, as they are possibly the best-flavored parts.

Warnings/Comments: Some species of buttercup (*Ranunculus* spp.) may have somewhat similar foliage, but a taste test and attention to characteristics will easily differentiate the two. There are 5 recognized wild varieties of cut-leaved coneflower, though many commercial cultivar varieties are available. Often planted in flower gardens, the flowers are a good nectar source for late pollinators such as butterflies and bumblebees. Coneflower is another confusing common name that represents plants of at least 3 genera: *Echinacea*, *Rudbeckia*, and *Ratibida*.

CUP ROSINWEED (AKA CARPENTER DOCK)
Silphium perfoliatum

Edible parts/harvest time: Meristems and leaves in late spring and early summer. Seeds in early fall. Native.

I've known this plant since childhood but was recently introduced to its edibility by Alan Bergo in his excellent blog and book (*The Forager Chef*). It is a strong-flavored plant not covered in most resources but has excellent culinary properties when properly prepared.

Description: A tall perennial up to 10' tall with unbranched square stems and numerous yellow flowers resembling sunflowers. The root system consists of a central taproot and abundant shallow rhizomes, often forming large colonies. Flowering stems are smooth, stout, and 4-edged with sharp corners. Opposite leaves are up to 1' long, oval to triangular, with wavy, coarsely toothed margins. Leaf blades have numerous raised dots on both surfaces, giving them a rough feel. The leaf bases surround the stem and form a cup

Meristem at collection stage

that will hold water, thus the name. Blooms July–September, with a panicle of flowering stems forming at the stem apex. Individual flowers are about 3–4" across, consisting of numerous yellow disk florets surrounded by 18–40 yellow ray florets. The ray florets are fertile and produce thin achenes, each with a well-developed marginal wing for wind distribution. Many plants in the genus are referred to as rosinweeds, due to the sticky sap that exudes from torn or broken foliage. This sap can be dried and used as chewing gum.

Habitat/Range: Occurs in moist black-soil prairies, cropland borders, low-lying woodland edges and thickets, bottomlands, fens and seeps, borders of ponds and lakes, fencerows, waste areas, and ditches near roadways and railroads. Range is the central United States from northeastern Oklahoma and the easternmost parts of Kansas to South Dakota, east to the Great Lakes region. Scattered populations exist elsewhere.

Uses: Cup rosinweed has a moderately strong flavor resembling Sochan, and it mixes well with other milder greens or when cooked or added to cooked dishes. The tender top leaves and young stem (meristem) will be milder in flavor than larger leaves and can be blanched and/or sautéed for use in salads. Larger leaves can enclose other foods for steaming. The seeds resemble wild sunflower seeds in flavor but are a bit smaller. The large, stout stems have a soft pithy center that can be hollowed out, then the stem is fire-hardened and used for a blowgun. The cups at the leaf bases can accumulate enough rainwater to be used as an emergency water source.

Warnings/Comments: There are around a half-dozen species of *Silphium* found in prairie habitats; many have showy flowers and are used in ornamental or pollinator-friendly flower gardens. Because of their strong flavor and tough foliage, most aren't edible except for the sunflower-like seeds.

ASTERACEAE SUBFAMILY CICHORIEAE (DANDELION TRIBE)

A subfamily of Asteraceae, this tribe is home to many edible species. All exude a milky latex when torn or broken.

CHICORY (AKA BLUE SAILORS)
Cichorium intybus

Chicory greens at collection stage

Edible parts/harvest time: Leaves, flowers in late spring through summer but are milder in winter. Basal rosette leaves and root is best harvested in fall before the first frost. Introduced.
Description: This common perennial is up to 3' tall, with stiff, erect branching stems that are grooved and somewhat hairy. Alternate leaves are up to 8" long and 2" across, becoming smaller as they ascend the stem. Lower leaves have a prominent central vein with hairs along the underside; margins are pinnatifid to sharply dentate, sometimes with broad, deep sinuses. Small upper leaves are usually lanceolate and sessile, with smooth margins. Leaves bleed milky sap when torn. Blooms May–October, with 2–3 pale to bright blue flowers occurring at leaf axils along the stem, or at the stem terminus. Each flower is 1–1½" across, consisting of a corolla with several pale blue stamens and blue anthers at the center, and 12–15 radial, narrow petals, each with 5 tiny teeth at the tips.

Habitat/Range: Found mostly in open, disturbed ground, in fields, pastures, waste areas, abandoned lots, and along roadsides and railroads. Range is throughout the United States and Canada, native to Europe. **Uses:** Dandelion, chicory, and their relatives tend to be somewhat bitter, less so when collected early or when basal rosettes reappear in late fall. Young, tender leaves and flowers are good salad ingredients when mixed with milder greens. They can be boiled as a potherb, or blanched and seasoned after discarding the water to use in cooked dishes. Soaking overnight in water may remove some bitterness. The young roots of chicory and dandelion are edible when boiled in 1 or more waters, but they are most well-known as "Cajun Coffee" when roasted and ground as a coffee substitute or additive.

Chicory flowers

Warnings/Comments: Cultivated varieties of chicory greens are grown around the world and sold under the names Belgian endive, escarole, and radicchio. Many of these cultivars produce larger, milder leaves and larger roots than their wild counterparts.

WILD LETTUCE
Lactuca canadensis and others

Edible parts/harvest time: Young basal leaves and tops in spring through summer. Native and introduced.

Description: Wild lettuce is an herbaceous biennial emerging as a basal rosette, with a second-year green to reddish smooth flower stalk to 8' tall. Alternate leaves are variable, pale or dark green, occasionally purplish, mostly lanceolate-oblong, with soft hairs on the midrib. Larger leaves are up to 10" long and 3" wide, with deep, pinnate lobes and sparsely toothed margins. Smaller leaves have shallower lobes or are unlobed. Blooms August–October, with small, yellow or pale orange, dandelion-like flowers appearing on a narrow panicle at the stem terminus, each becoming a seedhead with a fluff of pappus bristles. The plant exudes a tan or pale orange latex when torn.

Prickly lettuce

Prickly lettuce (*L. serriola*) is a similar Eurasian species but with clasping, pale bluish-green leaves, stiff prickles along the leaf margins and midribs, and a white latex. Florida lettuce (*L. floridana*) has blue flowers and white latex, occasionally with unlobed leaves, and is found in more wooded habitats.

Habitat/Range: Found in glades, thickets, savannas, openings in woodlands, pond and lake borders, riverbanks, fencerows, pastures, old fields, power line cuts, roadsides, and vacant lots. Common in disturbed ground, occasionally in pristine habitats. Range is the eastern half of the United States. Prickly lettuce is found throughout the United States.

Uses: Flavor varies in *Lactuca* species and in individual plants. Some are mild, while some are quite bitter, and more so with age. *L. canadensis* seems to be the mildest. Harvest when second-year emerging stalks sprout bunches of early growth leaves, as they are tender and mild for salad greens. Older leaves can be boiled as a potherb or mixed with milder greens. Latex of *Lactuca* species is used externally to treat poison ivy rash and other skin irritations. Older sources report mild sedative properties when dried to make lettuce "opium" (lactucarium); however, no supporting scientific evidence of a sedative compound has been found. It has been used in calming syrups and teas, and to treat coughs and upper-respiratory distress.

Canada lettuce flowers

Warnings/Comments: First cultivated in ancient Egypt, our domestic lettuce varieties are descendants of *L. serriola*—another instance where selective breeding removed the bitterness of native species, along with many of the health benefits. A shining example is the ever-present iceberg lettuce, which is basically crunchy water. It is minimally nutritious and lacks in vitamins and minerals when compared to its wild counterparts.

PERENNIAL SOW THISTLE
Sonchus arvensis and others

Edible parts/harvest time: Leaves in spring and early summer. Flowers and buds as soon as they appear. Introduced.

Description: A winter or spring annual up to 3' tall, usually with an erect, solitary stem that only branches near the terminus when flowers appear. Alternate leaves are up to 8" long and 2¼" across, becoming smaller and sparser as they ascend the central stem. Leaf blades are odd-pinnate with deep triangular lobes; margins are dentate with soft spines. The upper leaves can be entire or have shallow lobes. Yellow ray flowers similar to dandelion form in tight clusters at the stem terminus; each flower is up to 1¼" across. All parts exude a milky latex when torn. Common sow thistle (*S. oleraceus*) is similar but with smaller flowers. Spiny sow thistle (*S. asper*) tends to have shiner leaves with fewer lobes and has more aggressive spines on the margins.

Habitat/Range: Prefers open conditions and disturbed ground, in pastures, fields, roadsides, gardens, yards, vacant lots, near buildings, and in waste areas. Native to Eurasia, all three Sonchus species occur throughout most of North America and southern Canada.

Uses: Resembling a taller, pricklier version of a dandelion, sow thistle leaves and flower buds are a great addition to cooked greens. Cooking softens the prickles and improves the slightly bitter flavor. Fresh flowers are good in salads. Pickle unopened flower buds in vinegar, salt, and spices to make capers. Like all in the dandelion tribe, the young roots are edible and can be ground and roasted for a coffee stretcher or substitute (no caffeine, so what's the point?).

Warnings/Comments: Sow thistle is an aggressive disturbed-ground colonizer considered to be an agricultural pest in some areas.

DANDELION
Taraxucum officinale and others

Edible parts/harvest time: Leaves, buds and flowers in spring, summer, or whenever present. Roots in late fall to spring. Introduced.

Dandelion is possibly the most recognized plant wherever it occurs, primarily known to Americans as a lawn pest. Brought here by European settlers as a food source, it is highly prized by foragers as a vitamin-packed salad green, potherb, or coffee substitute.

Description: A low-growing perennial consisting of a basal rosette with oblanceolate, triangular-toothed leaves emerging from a taproot, and singly borne bright yellow ray flowers 1–1½" across, each on a slender, hollow stem up to 16" tall. The flower matures into a small, round seedhead embedded with tiny, elongated achenes, each with a long, slender beak attached to a tuft of parachute-like pappus bristles. This forms the familiar round "blowballs" that enable wind distribution. All parts of the plant exude a white latex when broken.

Habitat/Range: Found in a wide variety of open, disturbed areas, commonly near human habitation. Occurs in lawns, gardens, meadows, vacant lots, roadsides, waste areas, and cropland borders. Native of Eurasia, adventive throughout the United States and Canada.

Uses: Young, tender leaves are great mixed with milder salad greens and can be cooked as a potherb or added to any dish where a slight bitter element is desired. Hold an open flower at the base, then pinch and roll it between your fingers to push the tasty yellow petals and center out from the bitter green sepals for an attractive salad garnish. Flowers can be fried in batter for fritters or used to make wine or syrup after removing the sepals. If collected before they become bitter, very young taproots can be boiled and eaten, or can be dried, ground, and roasted for a coffee substitute or additive. My favorite use is to make dandelion root syrup by reducing a strong root tea with sugar. It tastes a bit like an alcohol-free Kahlua and has various culinary uses. The whole plant has been used medicinally for various ailments.

Warnings/Comments: Dandelion is a member of a large tribe of similar species, most of which are edible with similar uses. Many look-alikes are natives, referred to as false dandelions. Carolina false dandelion (*Pyrrhopappus carolinianus*) and potato false dandelion (*Krigia dandelion*) are edible but less common. The latter is named for its tasty round tubers. Due to their aggressive, colonizing nature, millions of dollars are spent annually to eliminate dandelions from lawns and croplands, yet they are cultivated and grown commercially for culinary and other uses in many countries.

DANDELION FLOWER SYRUP

This is a 2-day process.

1½ cups dandelion flowers (about 120 flowers)

2½ cups water

¼ cup raw honey

2 cups cane sugar

½ lemon, juiced

1. Day 1: Harvest flowers early while still open, then lay on a towel or flat surface outside to let bugs escape.

2. Remove the bitter calyx (the green part) by cutting it off with scissors. Alternate methods are to hold the calyx between the fingers of one hand and twisting off the yellow petals with the other, or pinch and roll the calyx between the finger and thumb, squeezing out the petals. Too many remaining green parts can make the syrup bitter.

3. Add petals and water to a pot, and simmer for about a minute.

4. Remove from heat, allow to cool, then place in a cool place or fridge to steep overnight.

5. Day 2: Strain the liquid into a fine-mesh strainer or a cheesecloth over a bowl. Extract as much liquid as possible by pushing the flowers against the mesh with a spoon or your fingers, or by squeezing and twisting the cheesecloth.

6. Add the strained liquid to a pot with the honey, sugar, and lemon. Bring to a boil, then lower the heat and simmer uncovered for about an hour, or until the liquid has reduced to the desired consistency; check by dipping a spoon in the syrup and letting it cool. Optimally, it is reduced roughly by half, but some prefer it thinner or thicker.

7. Pour into lidded glass jars or bottles and store refrigerated.

GOATSBEARD (AKA WILD SALSIFY)
Tragopogon dubius

Edible parts/harvest time: Leaves and roots in late spring and summer before they become tough. Buds and flowers as soon as they appear. Introduced.

Description: This biennial emerges as a rosette of basal leaves during the first year, then produces 1 or more flowering stalks about 1–3' tall. Alternate leaves are up to 1' long and ¾" wide, linear-lanceolate, with smooth margins. The leaves have parallel venation and strongly clasp the stem at its base, becoming smaller as they ascend the stems. Both stems and leaves are pale grayish green or bluish green and contain a white milky latex. The upper stems terminate in long, naked flowering stalks, each producing a single yellow flower about 2" across. The flowers produce a round seedhead about 3" across that looks like a giant dandelion blowball.

Habitat/Range: Found in pastures, cropland borders, dry meadows, vacant lots, waste areas, and along railroads and roadsides. Prefers disturbed ground habitats. Range is across much of the United States, except for the Southeast.

Uses: The entire plant is edible; the cultivated form is said to have an oyster-like flavor. Young roots are eaten raw in salads, or are boiled, baked, and sautéed once mature. They can be added to soups or are grated and made into cakes. Older tough roots can be used for broth. The flower buds and flowers are added to salads or preserved by pickling.

Warnings/Comments: Excessive consumption of the root may result in abdominal discomfort, bloating, and diarrhea. Abide by the old saying: everything in moderation (even moderation).

Goatsbeard seedhead

BETULACEAE (BIRCHES, HAZELNUTS)

A family of 6 genera in about 167 species distributed in temperate and subarctic areas of the Northern Hemisphere, where some reach the northern limit of woody plants. Most are trees and shrubs, several of which are nut-bearing. Also included are alders, hornbeams, hazel-hornbeams, and hop-hornbeams.

AMERICAN HAZELNUT
Corylus americana

Edible parts/harvest time: Nuts in late summer and fall. Native.

Description: A thicket-forming, medium-size shrub to 12' tall. Bark is brown to grayish brown, smooth on younger stems, becoming rougher with age. Alternate, simple leaves are 2½–6" long, oval to ovate, with coarse double-serrate margins and hairy undersides. Male and female flowers form February–April on the same shrub. Male flowers are yellowish, cylindrical drooping catkins; inconspicuous female flowers form at swollen buds on the stem, with only the red stigmas showing. Nuts form in small green clusters from female flowers, with each ½–¾" nut surrounded by two papery, ragged-edged bracts, ripening to brown in July–early September. Nutshells are brown with a small pale disk at the attachment to the bract; nutmeats are white with brown skin.

Habitat/Range: Found in a variety of soils and conditions, including dry prairies, savannas, thickets, rocky wooded slopes, open woodlands, and along fencerows and semi-wooded roadway edges. Range is the easternmost parts of the central grasslands and scattered locations in Nebraska and the Dakotas.

Uses: The sweet nutmeats can be shelled and eaten raw, but they taste better after drying and roasting. Use generally as you would other nuts. Chop to use in breads, salads, and desserts, make nut milk to drink or for flavoring in coffee and cooked dishes, or grind to flour as an ingredient in nut/seedcakes. Straight, unbranched stems are great for making arrow shafts.

Warnings/Comments: Filberts (*C. maxima*) are a Eurasian species that is cultivated and sold commercially.

BRASSICACEAE (MUSTARDS)

This economically important family contains 4,060 species in 372 genera. The European species *Brassica oleracea* was selectively bred or altered over time to produce six of the most popular vegetables in the family. Each alteration produced a different vegetable by developing a different plant part, as follows: cabbage, terminal leaf buds; brussels sprouts, lateral leaf buds; kale, leaves; kohlrabi, stem; broccoli, stem and flower buds; cauliflower, flower buds. The family also includes other cruciferous vegetables, such as collards, radishes, turnips, and rutabagas. All forms have characteristic four-petaled flowers.

WINTERCRESS (AKA YELLOW ROCKET)
Barbarea vulgaris

Wintercress in bloom with seeds

Edible parts/harvest time: Shoots and flower buds in spring. Basal leaves in early spring or late fall. Introduced.

Description: A leafy, branched biennial up to 2" tall. The first-year basal rosette is up to 1' across; 1 or more flowering stalks appear the second year. Basal leaves are on long petioles, with opposite lateral lobes and a larger, ovate terminal lobe. Blade surface is shiny dark green; margins are undulate to shallowly lobed. Alternate leaves on the flower stalk are bluntly toothed, becoming smaller and sessile as they ascend the stem. Blooms April–June, forming bunches of small, yellow, 4-petaled flowers at each stem terminus. Flowers mature to produce slender, cylindrical seeds called siliques.

Habitat/Range: Found in cultivated or fallow fields, pastures, gardens, vacant lots, and along roadsides, streams, and railroads. Prefers open, disturbed areas. Range is the eastern half of Oklahoma, Kansas, and Nebraska; it has naturalized in scattered locations over much of the United States.

Uses: This plant leans toward the bitter side; soaking the greens in water overnight will remove some of the bitterness if desired. Young basal rosette leaves can be found in spring, late fall, and occasionally in winter, and are a dandy boiled green. Young shoots and the

Basal leaves at collection stage

tender ends of second-year stems are also good but may get bitter as they mature. Occasionally young flower buds are mild enough to eat raw; they taste like broccoli.

Warnings/Comments: Studies show that consuming large amounts of this plant may interfere with kidney function, but it would probably take more than one would eat in a single serving.

SHEPHERD'S PURSE
Capsella bursa-pastoris

Edible parts/harvest time: All green parts any time they are present and still tender. Roots are best in midsummer. Introduced.

Description: A summer or winter annual that forms a basal rosette with a single or sparsely branched flower stalk up to 2' tall. Basal leaves are lanceolate or oblanceolate, with deep pinnate lobes, up to 4½" long and ¾" wide. The main flower stalk and lower branches terminate in a raceme of tiny 4-petaled flowers, with a small, clasping lanceolate leaf at each branch axil. Each flower is less than ⅛" across, maturing into a two-lobed triangular or heart-shaped flattened seedpod on a slender, ascending pedicel. The flowering racemes elongate with age.

Habitat/Range: Found in nearly any disturbed, open habitat. Occurs in lawns, gardens, vacant lots, roadsides, pastures, and fields. A native of Europe, it is found throughout the United States and Canada, and it is one of the most widespread plants on the planet due to anthropogenic distribution.

Uses: Young pre-flowering basal leaves, tender stem tops, flowers, and seedpods are a great salad addition, with a broccoli-like flavor. Older leaves become peppery but can be boiled as a potherb or used in cooked dishes. The root can be boiled as a vegetable or dried and ground for a ginger substitute. Widely used as a medicinal for numerous ailments.

Warnings/Comments: As with many plants, consumption of large quantities isn't advised. Reported symptoms from overconsumption are drowsiness, changes in blood pressure, thyroid function changes, heart palpitations, and miscarriages during pregnancy, although I suspect one would have to eat a bellyful to experience these symptoms.

PEPPERGRASS (AKA FIELD CRESS, PENNYCRESS, POOR MAN'S PEPPER)
Lepidium virginicum and others

Edible parts/harvest time: Greens in late spring to summer. Tops, roots, and seeds in summer to fall. Native and introduced.

Description: Low-growing basal rosette leaves are up to 3" long and have pinnate lobes resembling dandelion leaves. The flowering stem is up to 15" tall, with alternate stem leaves that are ovate to slender, with entire to toothed margins. The upper stem branches into cylindrical, flowering racemes up to 4" long (like a small bottlebrush), with small 4-petaled flowers, typical of mustards. Flowers mature to flattened, oval to round seeds, often with a small cleft at the tip.

Several *Lepidium* species are found in the prairie region; the most common are the natives *L. virginicum* and *L. densiflorum*. Field pennycress (*Thlaspi arvense*) is an edible introduced species also referred to as peppergrass.

Habitat/Range: Occurs in open, disturbed ground, fields, pastures, roadsides, lawns, gardens, and vacant lots. *L. virginicum* is common throughout the United States, less common in the northern plains. *L. densiflorum* is less common in the Southeast. *Thlaspi arvense* is found in the northern two-thirds of the United States.

Uses: The seeds taste like black pepper and can be used to flavor meats, soups, and other cooked dishes. Flowers and young leaves can be added raw to salads and are especially tasty when paired with wood or field sorrel leaves for a lemon-pepper flavoring. The seeds can be ground for a pepper substitute. The young root can be eaten raw as a trail nibble, or ground and mixed with vinegar for a horseradish substitute.

Warnings/Comments: A few allergic reactions have been reported; sample cautiously before consuming any quantity. Around 170 *Lepidium* species occur globally, with approximately 56 in North America.

Field pennycress

WATERCRESS
Nasturtium officinale

Edible parts/harvest time: Top leaves and stems above the waterline, in early to late spring before flowering. Introduced.

This was my mom's favorite wild salad green, gathered at the nearby Okino Dairy Farm where it still grows abundantly at the springhouse milk cooler. The water was certainly contaminated from the large pasture atop the hill and occasional cows that got into the spring, but it never bothered us. Maybe because the hot bacon grease and vinegar she put on decontaminated it, or possibly because our 50-foot-deep well never passed a water test and we were used to it.

Description: This low-growing aquatic perennial often forms large mats in shallow springs, seeps, and along cold-water streambanks. Long rootlets along the stem at leaf nodes allow it to root into mud or gravel bottoms, where it forms dense colonies that can often grow to a height of 1' above the water's surface. Alternate leaves are clasping, bipinnately compound, 3–6" long, with 3–9 leaflets, usually with a rounded leaflet at the top and several opposite, rounded leaflets along the leaf axil. White flowers appear in April, forming in clusters on short-stemmed racemes at the tips of stems; each is 4 petaled and around ¼" across. Seedpods are long and thin, typical of many mustards. Several species of *Rorippa* are present in the central grasslands and are also referred to as various types of cress.

Habitat/Range: Found in flowing, cold water of springs and spring branches, seeps, fens, spring-fed marshes, and streambanks. Occasionally roots in soil. Occurs throughout North America, originally native to Eurasia. Widely distributed globally due to cultivation.

Uses: A nutritious and popular salad green known for its pungent, peppery flavor and numerous health benefits. It is best raw as a salad green but can be used as a steamed vegetable or added to soups or other cooked dishes to spice up the flavor. Best harvested before flowering unless you're fond of sharp, bitey flavors. Seeds can be sprouted, and shoots can be harvested days after germination. Used medicinally for various ailments.

Warnings/Comments: Always collect from a few inches above the waterline to avoid bacteria and parasites like liver flukes and *Giardia*, then wash well to avoid possible *E. coli* contamination. Rinse in vinegar water or give it a quick blanch if water quality is questionable. Studies have identified more than 15 essential vitamins and minerals in watercress, more iron than spinach, more calcium than milk, and more vitamin C than oranges. It is grown hydroponically and cultivated around the world, becoming increasingly available at supermarkets

TALL HEDGE MUSTARD
Sisymbrium loselii and others

Edible parts/harvest time: Greens in late spring and summer. Seeds in late summer. Introduced, invasive.

Description: This annual herb first emerges as a basal rosette typical of many mustards, then produces a hairy, erect stem that can exceed 3¼' in height. Alternate leaves are on short petioles, triangular to lanceolate, pinnately lobed or divided into 3–9 lobes. Leaf margins are smooth to toothed. Small, bright yellow flowers form on terminal racemes of flowers. The fruit is a silique up to 1⅓" long containing tiny seeds.

Tumble mustard (*S. altissimum*) has similar uses and is an upright, wispy-looking plant with slender, many-branched stems, growing to a roundish bush up to 5' tall. It forms as a basal rosette with broad, deeply pinnate lower leaves and thinner upper leaves. Stem leaves are divided into thin, linear lobes. It has a long blooming time, with inconspicuous 4-petaled yellow flowers around ¼" inch wide. Fruits are slender siliques up to 3" long. At maturity it dies, uproots, and tumbles in the wind for seed dispersal.

Tumble mustard, with basal rosette (inset) MATT LAVIN, WIKIMEDIA COMMONS

Habitat/Range: Occurs in pastures, croplands, roadsides, and waste places. Prefers open, sandy or rocky ground. Range is scattered locations throughout the northern and western half of the United States, absent in the Southeast.

Uses: Both basal and stem leaves can be used for salad greens or potherbs, best collected when young and tender. Collect ripe seeds in late summer and fall for use as flavoring in lacto-ferments and pickling. They can be mixed with other seeds for seedcakes and flour or made into a fine mustard condiment.

Warnings/Comments: This plant is often found near croplands and is possibly susceptible to pesticide/herbicide runoff. In my opinion, potential exposure by eating a few helpings of foraged plants found in these conditions is probably less than exposure from daily consumption of domestic plants from the grocery store (unless you can afford all-organic, and that still doesn't mean chemical-free).

CACTACEAE (CACTI)

A mostly new-world family consisting of 1,866 species in 131 genera. Most cacti are adapted to arid environments, although several species are native to rainforests and other tropical or subtropical areas. Many have succulent photosynthetic stems and reduced leaves that are often modified as spines; most have showy, many-petaled flowers.

PLAINS PRICKLY PEAR (AKA TWISTSPINE OR BIGROOT PRICKLY PEAR)
Opuntia macrorhiza and others

Edible parts/harvest time: Young, tender pads in late spring and early summer. Fruits and seeds in late summer through fall. Native.

This prairie native can be used similarly to the large western species and thornless cultivars popular in Mexican cuisine. Nopales (pads) and tunas (fruits) are occasionally found in supermarkets.

Description: A low-growing cactus up to 14" tall with succulent, ovoid or paddle-shaped pads up to 7" long and 5" wide, each dotted with areoles (air pores) in sparse rows. Each areole contains a tuft of brown, woolly hairs with tiny, sharp bristles (glochids) and 1–6 longer, stiff spines. Blooms June–July with 1 to several buds forming at the top of mature pads. Showy, yellow flowers are up to 3" across, each with numerous central stamens and many tepals; the innermost tepals often show a reddish-orange blotch. In late summer, flowers are replaced by pear-shaped purplish fruits up to 1½" long, each with a concave depression at the top and sparse tufts of glochidia on the outer surface. Fruits contain several roundish seeds, surrounded by sweet greenish or purplish flesh. Eastern prickly pear (*O. humifusa*) is similar with a more eastern range; it tends to sprawl or lie flat.

Habitat/Range: Occurs in dry, open habitats on glades, bluff tops, and ledges, dry benches along rivers, near exposed bedrock in upland or sand prairies, in rocky pastures, and along roadsides and railroads. Range is from Texas north to Nebraska and southern South Dakota, west to Arizona and southern Utah, and scattered locations to the east and west.

Uses: Very young pads can be eaten raw or cooked after removing glochidia and are best harvested before spines develop. Older pads can be peeled and the tough edges trimmed off. The flesh is somewhat mucilaginous. Harvest with thick gloves or tongs, then remove spines and glochidia by burning off by flame or by rubbing in sand and rinsing thoroughly. Glochidia can become airborne; use caution. Pads are good flame-roasted, sliced thin and used like string beans, fried like onion rings, or used in any cooked dish when a thickener is desired. The tunas have delicious, sweet-tart flesh that is good raw as a trail nibble or can be collected for use in syrups, jams, jellies, sauces, beverages, or wines. Remove the hard seeds; they can be roasted and ground for use as a flour additive. The gel-like juice from pads is used similarly to aloe vera to treat burns and skin conditions.

Warnings/Comments: Be thorough in cleaning both pads and fruits, as missed glochids are not fun when embedded in your tongue.

Prickly pear tunas ROCKY HOLLOW

GRILLED PRICKLY PEAR TACOS

Corn or flour tortillas

Filling

1 teaspoon cumin

Dash of garlic powder

1 (16-ounce) can black beans or 2 cups domestic or wild beans, cooked

6–8 young, thoroughly cleaned prickly pear pads

1 small onion, sliced into ½-inch-thick rounds

1–2 jalapeños, sliced in half with seeds removed

1 tablespoon olive oil

Salt to taste

Topping

2 cups finely sliced red cabbage and/or zesty wild greens

1 tablespoon lime juice

½ cup chopped cilantro

½ cup cotija or other dry cheese

1. In a small pan, heat beans. Add cumin and garlic powder; salt to taste and set aside.

2. Add lime juice and cilantro to sliced cabbage or greens; salt to taste and set aside.

3. Drizzle pads, onion, and jalapeños with olive oil; grill until slightly charred. A flat grill can be used, but grilling over an open wood flame is the bomb for this dish. Salt to taste, then slice all into taco-friendly strips.

4. Heat or lightly grill tortillas. Place a line of filling, black beans, cabbage topping, and cheese in the center.

5. Serve with chips and salsa. For the full ride, serve with roasted ground cherry/tomato salsa (see entry for ground cherry) and pair with a sumac margarita (see entry for sumac) flavored with prickly pear fruit syrup.

CANNABACEAE (CANNABIS, HACKBERRIES, HOPS)

This family has about 170 species grouped into 11 genera and can appear as trees, herbs or vines. One of these herbs has recently become a powerful economic driver in some states.

COMMON HACKBERRY
Celtis occidentalis and others

Edible parts/harvest time: Fruits in late summer through fall, may persist into winter. Native.

Hackberry fruits could be described as a nut/fruit hybrid; they have a thin skin of sweet flesh covering a hard-shelled seed with an oily and nutlike center.

Description: A straight-trunked tree with a rounded crown, up to 80' tall. The bark is mostly smooth and gray when young, developing distinctive warty projections and corky ridges with age. Alternate leaves are broadly to narrowly ovate, with an asymmetrical base, serrated margins, and a pointed tip. Flowers April–May, with male, female, and perfect flowers on the same tree. Flowers are yellow green and are ¼" across. In September–October, female flowers mature into round, purplish-black to orange drupes up to ½" across. Each drupe contains a seed with a round, hard shell, surrounded by a thin layer of somewhat dry flesh. Three other *Celtis* species occur in the central grasslands. Sugarberry (*C. laevigata*) is a bottomland species with narrower leaves and larger fruits, and a more southern range. Dwarf hackberry (*C. tenuifolia*) is generally shorter and shrub-like, found mostly in glades and dry, open habitats. Netleaf hackberry (*C. reticulata*) resembles dwarf hackberry but with more prominent net-like leaf veins. It occurs in central Texas, Oklahoma, and Kansas to many western states.

Habitat/Range: Found in bottomlands, moist upland slopes, savannahs, fencerows, and riverbanks. Prefers rich soil but will grow in many soil conditions. Range is from southern Oklahoma to the Dakotas and scattered locations farther west, and throughout the eastern United States.

Hackberry bark

Oily nutmeat inside hackberry seed

Uses: The berry flesh makes a nice trail nibble, but the edible and nutritious fleshy seed interior is the real treasure. The woody covering of the seed is hard enough to break a tooth! The whole crushed berries can be used in various ways. Put them in a dehydrator for a couple days, then pulverize in a spice grinder, sift, and cook with water to make nut milk. See recipe below for other processing tips.

Warnings/Comments: As mentioned above, biting the seeds may be hazardous to teeth. Hackberries were found with the remains of Peking Man (*Homo erectus*) that were dated to 500,000 years ago, possibly making it the first record of plant use by *Homo* spp.

NO-COOK HACKBERRY CANDY BARS

Famed forager/author Euell Gibbons made this treat as his first foraged recipe at age 5.

4–5 cups ripe hackberries

1 tablespoon honey or maple syrup

½ cup nuts, crushed (preferably wild nuts like pecan or hazelnut, but any will do)

½ cup dried fruits or berries, finely chopped

1. Use a mortar and pestle or molcajete to thoroughly pulverize the whole fruits. Take your time on this step; the longer you work at it, the less chance of later encountering the woody hull fragments. The fruit flesh and oily meat inside the seeds will give the mush a stiff cookie dough–like texture, and it's quite tasty at this stage.

2. To make no-cook candy bars, add the honey, crushed nuts, and chopped fruits. Mix well, then roll out thinly between layers of parchment paper or plastic wrap. Allow to dry, then cut into desired shapes and sizes for storage.

3. **Note:** The finished product may contain tiny seed hull fragments that are easily avoided by not biting down too hard while chewing. To avoid the woody bits entirely, put the crushed fruits in a pan with a bit of water and simmer while stirring to loosen the flesh and soften the seeds. Squeeze through a fine strainer or cheesecloth to remove the hull remnants.

Hackberry candy bars

CARYOPHYLLACEAE
(CHICKWEEDS, CARNATIONS, PINKS)

This large, mostly herbaceous family has 2,625 known species in 81 genera. Many are cultivated as ornamental garden flowers; a few species, such as common chickweed, are considered to be pests and weeds.

COMMON CHICKWEED
Stellaria media and others

Edible parts/harvest time: Leaves and stems whenever tender growth is present. Introduced.

Description: A low-growing annual/perennial with weak, branching stems up to 1' long. Stems are often prostrate from the base, becoming erect at the upper portion. Color is light green to occasionally burgundy, with a single, linear row of small hairs. Pairs of opposite leaves occur along the stems; leaves are ovate to deltoid, up to 1" long and ¾" wide but usually smaller. Leaves have petioles on lower pairs but are sessile on upper pairs. Small flowers occur on cymes at the branch tips, each ¼" across with a pale green central ovary; the 5 white petals are so deeply cleft as to appear as 10 petals. Long-leaved starwort (*S. longifolia*) is similar but with long, slender leaves up to 2" long and larger, longer-petaled flowers up to ⅓" across. Mouse-ear chickweed (*Cerastium fontanum*) is similar but with rounded, hairy leaves. Several similar species are referred to as chickweed, starwort, or stitchwort; all are edible.

Habitat/Range: Occurs in mostly moist soil or disturbed ground in lawns, gardens, croplands, bottomlands, near springs and ponds, and in rich soil near streambanks, damp meadows, and waste areas. Native to Eurasia and introduced throughout the United States and Canada. Found almost globally due to anthropogenic distribution.

Uses: Young, tender tops and leaves are good raw as a mild salad green; chop up older stems to avoid the stringiness. They can be steamed or used as a spinach substitute in pesto, breads, quiche, soups, and other cooked dishes. They don't hold up well to much cooking, so add during the last few minutes.

Warnings/Comments: Chickweeds contain saponins that can cause gastric distress in some people when eaten in large quantities. In winter, look for clumps of chickweed and several other edibles around protected areas near springs, bases of slopes, or under piles of leaf litter. It will pop up nearly any time of year with adequate moisture and several days of above-freezing temps.

CLEOMACEAE (BEEPLANTS, SPIDER PLANTS)

Cleomaceae are a small family of flowering plants in the order Brassicales (mustards), comprising about 300 species in 10 genera. Thirteen genera and 35 species are found in the United States, mostly with quite limited distribution; the two most widespread genera are *Peritoma* and *Polanisia*.

ROCKY MOUNTAIN BEE PLANT (AKA STINKING CLOVER)
Peritoma and others

Edible parts/harvest time: Shoots and leaves in spring. Fruits and seeds in summer and early fall. Native.

Description: An attractive erect annual up to 5' tall; its distinctive showy flowers have very long, pale pink stamens with green tips, and the foliage has a somewhat disagreeable odor. Stems are smooth and hairless, with several to many erect branches. Compound, mostly trifoliate leaves are arranged in a spiral along the lower stems, becoming single as they near the flower bunches. Lower leaves are on long petioles, becoming shorter as they ascend the stem. Leaflets are 1–2½" long and around ½" inch wide, narrowly lanceolate-elliptic and pointed at the tip, with smooth to finely serrated margins. Blooms June–September, with rounded flower clusters forming at the tips of branches and fruits forming below. Flowers are ½" to nearly 2" across with 4 oblong petals that abruptly narrow near the base and are asymmetrically arranged. Color ranges from cream white to pink to purplish. Six long, straight, purple-tipped stamens up to 1" long protrude from the calyx. Fruits are drooping, elongated pods up to 2–3" long, each containing around 12 kidney-shaped seeds approximately ⅛" long. Redwhisker clammyweed/spiderflower (*Polanisia dodecandra*) is used similarly and has a similar growth/flower pattern with generally smaller leaves covered in sticky hairs. Its whitish flowers produce long, pinkish to red stamens, and its seedpods are held erect.

Redwhisker clammyweed

Habitat/Range: Prairies and grass-lands, open woods, foothills, and along roadsides. Prefers moist alkaline soils that are light or sandy, and dis-turbed ground. Range is from central Oklahoma to North Dakota in the east, and throughout the Mountain West from California to Washington. Scat-tered isolated populations exist from Iowa to the Great Lakes states.

Uses: Despite its strong flavor, parts of the plant can be eaten raw, cooked, or dried. Shoots and leaves are typi-cally eaten as a potherb but can be eaten raw when mixed with milder greens or dried for storage. Greens can be soaked in water overnight to subdue strong flavors, then boiled, mixed with other greens, or added to cooked dishes. The highly nutritious seeds can be eaten raw, cooked in soups, ground into flour, or added to other seeds or grains to make seedcakes and flat-cakes. The showy flowers are a great addition to salads. A yellow-green dye for coloring fabrics and pottery can be made by boiling the leaves, and a black dye is made by boiling the woody stems for an extended time. The plant is used medicinally for many ailments, both internally and externally.

Warnings/Comments: May be toxic to livestock if consumed in quantity. Seeds of both species have been recorded in archaeological excavations. Both natives and showy cultivars are pollinator magnets.

CONVOLVULACEAE (SWEET POTATOES, BINDWEEDS, AND MORNING GLORIES)

This family consists of about 60 genera with more than 1,650 species of trees, shrubs, herbs, and herbaceous vines. *Ipomoea* is the most numerous, with over 600 species including sweet potato (*I. betatas*) and other food tubers. Most have winding stems and a funnel-shaped, radially symmetrical corolla with five sepals, five fused petals, and stamens fused to the petals. Leaves are usually simple and alternate. Seeds of some morning glory species were used in making *ololiuhqui*, a somewhat psychoactive "divinatory" substance used by the Aztecs. They contain toxic ergoline alkaloids similar to LSD but with more dangerous side effects.

WILD POTATO VINE (AKA MANROOT)
Ipomoea pandurata and others

Edible parts/harvest time: Roots in fall to spring. Native.

Description: A perennial twining vine up to 20' long, with a mostly hairless green to reddish stem. Will readily climb adjacent structures and vegetation or sprawl in open areas. Alternate, cordate leaves occur singly at nodes on green or purplish petioles. Leaf blades are olive green, up to 6" long and 4" across, with smooth margins. Flower stalks form singly at leaf axils, with 1–7 flowers emerging as a terminal cluster on each stalk. Each flower has a funnel-shaped white corolla with a rose-pink or purplish coloration deep in the throat and 5 shallow lobes, and are 2½–3" across when fully open. Blooms May–September, with short-lived flowers emerging early in the morning or later in the day on cloudy days. The root develops large, elongated tubers, often over 2' long and weighing 20–30 pounds. Bush morning glory (*I. leptophylla*) is a long-lived drought-tolerant prairie species with similar uses to wild potato. Its stems are smooth and leafy, often prostrate or bending into an arc to form a bushy clump reaching about 3' in height. Delicate, alternate leaves are lanceolate to linear, up to 5" long, with smooth margins, usually upturned at the stem. Flowers resemble wild potato in size and shape but are pinkish to purplish in color, often deeper purple in the throat. Its tuber may grow to a huge size; one specimen recorded from Colorado was over 5' long.

Bush morning glory

Habitat/Range: Wild potato occurs in fencerows, thickets, old fields, croplands, edges of prairies near woodlands, banks of rivers, streams, ponds, and lakes, and along roadsides and railroads. Prefers disturbed areas but can also be found in pristine habitats. Range is eastern Texas, Oklahoma, and Kansas, north and east to Iowa and Pennsylvania, and south to central Florida. Considered to be a noxious weed in several states. Bush morning glory prefers open mixed-grass prairies with sandy, gravelly soil and has a more western range.

Uses: Young, tender roots can be sliced/cubed and roasted or boiled like potatoes; parboiling beforehand is useful if bitterness is present. One would assume they'd have a similar texture and flavor to their relative the sweet potato, but some describe the texture as more meat-like and reminiscent of a pork roast or steak. Older roots tend to be tough and bitter but can still be used when boiled in 2 or 3 waters to remove bitterness. (The bigger the root, the longer the boiling time.) They can then be seasoned and roasted or added to soups and other dishes. The root can also be sliced or cubed and dehydrated for later use; the bits rehydrate nicely. Old, dried roots were used by indigenous tribes as an ember-carrier; it was said to be able to keep an ember going for a month. The entire plant has extensive medicinal and ceremonial uses.

Warnings/Comments: Wild potato flowers may appear similar to toxic morning glories (*Convolvulus* spp.). Those species do not develop large tubers or have the rose coloring in the throat of the inflorescence. Several states ban the cultivation of some *Ipomoea* species as invasive pests. The seeds of some species may have psychoactive properties. Wild potato's showy flowers and ease of propagation make it popular as a garden ornamental.

Wild potato root

CUCURBITACEAE (GOURDS, SQUASH)

A family consisting of about 95 genera containing around 965 species found in the tropics and in temperate areas, where those with edible fruits were among the earliest cultivated plants in both the Old and New Worlds. The family Cucurbitaceae ranks among the highest of plant families for number and percentage of species used as human food.

BUFFALO GOURD
Cucurbita foetidissima

ROCKY HOLLOW

Edible parts/harvest time: Flowers in mid- to late summer. Seeds and roots in late summer to fall. Native.

Description: A perennial vine emerging from a large tuberous root, often deep in the ground. Enormous roots 4' in diameter and 170+ pounds have been recorded. Prostrate, ridged vines up to 20–30' long emerge from the root, often sprawling in several directions. Alternate, grayish-green leaves are triangular-ovate, up to 12" long and 5" wide at the base, on long petioles. They are often held at about a 45-degree angle. Leaf blades have a rough upper surface and are somewhat hairy below, with irregular teeth at the margins. Tendrils and large yellow-orange flowers on short peduncles appear at leaf axils. Flowers are 2–4" long, 5-lobed, with stamens that have large anthers deep inside the throat. Globular fruits are up to 4" across, green-striped when young and turning yellow at maturity. Each fruit contains numerous flattened, ovate seeds resembling small pumpkin seeds.

Habitat/Range: Occurs in dry, gravelly soils of rangelands, prairies, roadsides, fencerows, and ditch banks. Range is southern Nebraska south to central Texas, west to the southern half of California.

Uses: Seeds can be thoroughly cleaned and roasted with seasoning like pepitas, boiled, or ground into mush. The flesh of very young immature fruits is said to be edible after cooking,

but most specimens may be too bitter, especially as they age and the bitter saponins develop. The dryish fruit pulp and leaves can be crushed and vigorously rubbed between the hands with a bit of water to produce a field-expedient but somewhat low-quality soap. The root was processed into starch by some indigenous tribes.

Warnings/Comments: The mature fruits contain saponins and cucurbitacins that may potentially reach toxic levels in mature fruits. Less so with younger fruits, but do not consume if bitterness isn't removed by cooking or processing.

Buffalo gourds

CREEPING CUCUMBER
(AKA WILD CUCUMBER, MELONCITO)
Melothria pendula

MEREDITH MATTINGLY

Edible parts/harvest time: Unripe green fruits sporadically in May through October. Ripe purple fruits should not be eaten. Native.

Description: A climbing or spreading vine resembling a domestic cucumber, with slender, delicate stems and twining, unbranched tendrils. Alternate, simple leaves are generally heart shaped and palmately lobed with 3–5 simple lobes. The small yellow flowers are 5-lobed, appearing solitary or in small clusters at the leaf axils. The flowers mature to oblong or globoid green berries with light streaking or mottling, appearing like a tiny watermelon. They are about an inch long, ripen to purple, and contain many white seeds.

Habitat/Range: Occurs in floodplain forests, ditches, ravines, seeps, streambanks, roadsides, thickets, fencerows, moist sandy habitats, and disturbed ground. Range is Oklahoma and the eastern two-thirds of Texas, and scattered locations throughout the southeastern United States.

Uses: Unripe green fruits are delicious eaten raw like cucumbers, skin and all. The flavor is not unlike a cucumber but sweeter, perfect for salads. They can also be pickled in vinegar like cucumbers, lacto-fermented in salt brine, or made into wild cucumber relish. The green parts and fruits have a long history of medicinal uses.

Warnings/Comments: Ripe purplish-black fruits may have powerful laxative properties. The plant has a long fruiting season and may be found with flowers, green fruits, and ripe fruits on the same vine. According to Green Deane, studies have shown the fruits to be 12.6 percent protein, 16.30 percent fiber, and 56.8 percent carbohydrates.

RECIPE

SPICY WILD CUCUMBER RELISH WITH ROASTED RED PEPPERS AND ONIONS

2–3 cups green wild cucumbers

½ red bell pepper

½ medium-sized sweet onion

1 jalapeño pepper

Brine

2 cups sugar

2 cups cider vinegar (or homemade wild fruit vinegar)

1 tablespoon mustard seed

2 teaspoons celery seed

1 teaspoon ground turmeric

1. Slice peppers and onions into thin strips, and place on a foil-lined baking pan with the skins up. Roast or broil till everything has a bit of charred skin.

2. Coarsely chop roasted peppers and onion, quarter the fresh wild cucumbers.

3. Combine sugar and cider vinegar in a heavy stainless steel or nonstick pot, bring to a boil, and stir until the sugar dissolves. Add mustard and celery seeds and ground turmeric; reduce heat. Simmer 5 minutes, then add wild cucumbers and vegetables and simmer for another 5 minutes. Ladle the hot relish into hot, sterilized pint jars, leaving a ½-inch headspace. Wipe jar rims and add lids and screw bands.

EBENACEAE (PERSIMMONS, EBONIES)

This family of mostly trees and shrubs contains around 500 species in 4 genera. Several species are known for their beautiful wood; a few are cultivated for their fruits.

AMERICAN PERSIMMON
Diospyros virginiana

Edible parts/harvest time: Leaves for tea in spring and early summer. Fruits in September to November, best after the first frost but many will start to ripen earlier. Native.

Many kids in rural areas grew up gathering persimmons so our moms would make bread or pudding for dessert. When unknowing friends or relatives would come to visit in the fall (being the ornery brats we were), we'd find a tree with a few ripe fruits and eat one, saying how sweet it was, then hand them an unripe fruit to watch the fun! The astringent taste of unripe fruit sticks to the tongue with a high amount of pucker power, and I learned quickly not to do this to kids who were bigger or faster than I was.

Description: Persimmon trees can grow to 65' but are usually smaller, often fruiting at 10' tall. Simple alternate leaves are glossy and leathery with smooth margins, 2–6" long and 1–3" wide. Distinctive bark is dark colored and deeply grooved, with ridges broken into rectangular blocks. Small, fragrant, urn-shaped flowers appear in midsummer, each with 4 decurved white lobes. Smaller male flowers appear in clusters; solitary female flowers

up to ⅔" across mature to produce globe-shaped green fruits ¾–1½" across, each containing up to 6 flattened-oval seeds. Ripening begins in late September, when fruits turn orange with purplish hues. When fully ripe, they are soft and slightly wrinkled, and the skin has a translucent appearance. Many will not ripen to full sweetness until after a hard frost in October.

Habitat/Range: Found in prairies, old fields, glades, open dry woods, bottomlands, stream/forest edges, fencerows, and thickets. Occurs in the eastern half of Texas and Oklahoma, the eastern third of Kansas, and throughout the southeastern United States.

Uses: The sweet, ripe fruits are great on the spot. To process, press the fruits through a metal colander or chinois to remove the seeds and skins. Use the pulp in desserts, puddings, breads, sweet soups, and other dishes, or freeze for later. Spread a thin layer of pulp on wax paper or plastic wrap and dry to make fruit leather, or dry the fruits whole. Brandied persimmons are a great cordial, or use them to make beer, if that is your thing. The dried leaves make a great tea that is packed with antioxidants, and antiviral and anti-carcinogenic compounds. The dark heartwood has been used to make golf clubs and is highly regarded as a superior bow wood. It has similar valuable properties to its tropical relative, ebony.

Warnings/Comments: Unripe fruits are very astringent and unpalatable. According to folklore, splitting the seeds can predict the severity of the winter. The shape of the cotyledon either appears as a spoon (snow, severe conditions), knife (cutting, cold wind), or fork (mild winter). According to studies, the shape more likely reflects the severity of the previous winter. Japanese persimmon (*D. kaki*) is an Asian cultivar that is sold commercially.

RECIPE

PERSIMMON MOUSSE WITH CINNAMON CRUMBLE

Crumble

½ cup white flour

1 tablespoon butter

1 teaspoon powdered sugar

½ teaspoon cinnamon (or substitute your favorite spices)

Mousse

3 cups persimmon pulp, blended with a mixer or blender

2 cups whipped cream

Dash of lemon juice

¼ teaspoon vanilla

1. Mix crumble ingredients to a rough breadcrumb texture. Scatter on a flat pan and bake at low heat until lightly browned.

2. Gently mix mousse ingredients together until fluffy and smooth. ***Note:*** Other fruits or berries can be pulped and substituted for persimmon; whole blueberries or other fresh berries are a nice addition.

3. Serve mousse in pudding cups, topped with crumble. For the ubiquitous pumpkin spice version, forego the crumble and sprinkle cinnamon, nutmeg, ground clove, allspice, and ground ginger to taste. If you must.

ELAEAGNACEAE (SILVERBERRIES, OLEASTERS)

A small family with about 60 species in 3 genera; most have stems with thorns and simple leaves with scales or hairs. Several species are horticulturally important, and some are cultivated for their edible berries. Three native species of buffaloberry (*Shepherdia* spp.) in the United States have similar characteristics and edible berries. Introduced species such as Russian olive and autumn olive have become invasive pests.

SILVER BUFFALOBERRY
Shepherdia argentea and others

Edible parts/harvest time: Berries in July and August. Native.

Buffaloberry fruits are a nutritional and medicinal superfood rich in carotenoid and phenolic antioxidants. Like their invasive cousin autumn olive, they may contain up to 18 times more lycopene than tomatoes.

Description: A bushy and branching shrub up to 8' tall, occasionally growing to 18' and often forming large thickets. Many of the stems terminate in sharp thorns, making harvest somewhat difficult. The leaves are covered with pubescent silver scales, giving the plant a silvery appearance. Opposite leaves are elliptic, up to 2" long and ⅝" wide. Blooms in early spring before the leaves emerge. Tiny, tubular yellowish flowers, each with a 4-lobed calyx, form at the leaf axils. One-seeded, bright red fruits are produced by pollinated female flowers and are about ¼" across, round to ovate, appearing singly or in clusters along the stems.

Autumn olive (*Elagnus umbellata*) often has multiple spreading stems and grows to 20' tall. Its alternate leaves are up to 3" long and 1¼" across, elliptic-ovate with smooth wavy margins. Bark on smaller stems is grayish brown and smooth, often with lenticels and short thorns. Upper leaf surface is light green with sparse scales; undersides are pale green to whitish with dense silvery scales. Fruits are up to ⅓" across, pink to red at maturity, and finely dotted with silver scales. They are often produced in prodigious amounts. Autumn olive is used similarly to buffaloberry and is found in the easternmost parts of the central grasslands.

Habitat/Range: Occurs in a variety of habitats, including riparian areas along edges of floodplains, wet meadows, streams, rivers, lakes, and springs, and dry habitats such as prairies, woodlands, foothills, and open to partially wooded slopes. Range is from Kansas, Iowa, and Wisconsin west to California and Oregon.

Uses: Technically a stone fruit and not a berry, the ripe fruits can be eaten raw but are somewhat astringent. They are best used in syrups, pies, jellies, and sauces, or can be dried for storage or made into cakes for winter food. Indigenous tribes in the north used the berries for "Indian ice cream," a tart, frothy dessert made by beating/whisking buffaloberries with hot water sweetened with other berries, natural sweeteners, or later, sugar. The froth is a result of naturally occurring "lathering" saponins in the fruits.

Warnings/Comments: Saponins in the fruits can cause stomach distress or diarrhea when eaten raw in large quantities. Due to its copious fruit production,

Autumn olive berries

health benefits, and tolerance for poor soils and drier climates, buffaloberry is under consideration for commercial planting in tribal lands and other marginal habitats. It has also captured the attention of several commercial wine producers.

RECIPE

BUFFALOBERRY WHIP, AKA SXUSEM (SALISH) OR INDIAN ICE CREAM

2–3 cups buffaloberries

2 cups water

Sweeten with ¼ cup (or to taste) sugar, honey, agave nectar, or other sweet berries. Use stevia for a low-sugar option.

Optional: Cinnamon, nutmeg, or other spices used in desserts

Add ingredients to a clean metal bowl. Crush berries, then beat with a whisk or electric mixer into a frothy, mousse-like texture. Serve topped with strawberries, blueberries, or other sweet berries or fruits.

Traditionally, a whisk was made in the field by tying a small bundle of slender twigs together at one end; ingredients were then whisked in a pottery bowl or other open container. Alternately, put ingredients into a lidded container along with branched twigs or twisted wire to serve as a whisk, then shake vigorously for about 5 minutes.

FABACEAE (BEANS, PEAS, LEGUMES)

This large and economically important family harbors about 19,000 known species in 751 genera, second only to Poaceae (grasses) in its agricultural significance and percentage makeup of human diet. The family contains trees, shrubs, vines, and perennial or annual herbaceous plants, many of which are easily recognized by their characteristic pea flowers, legume fruits, and compound leaves.

LEADPLANT (AKA FALSE INDIGO, PRAIRIE SHOESTRINGS)
Amorpha canescens

Edible parts/harvest time: Leaves for tea as soon as they are present and before they become dry and tough. Native.

Description: A small, branching perennial 1–3' tall with 1 to several erect to sprawling stems; some stems develop tight, elongated spikes with showy lavender to purple flowers at their terminus. Stems are light green with white hairs, often becoming woody with age. Alternate, compound leaves are bipinnate, 4–12" long, and may have up to 50 small leaflets, each about ½" long and ¼" wide, with smooth margins and rounded or notched tips. Named for its fine, dull grayish hairs that often cover the plant, giving it the appearance of being dusted with lead, thus the name. Blooms May–August, with small flowers occurring along pubescent terminal spikes about 2–6" long at the ends of major branches. Individual purple flowers have a single upper petal that curls around conspicuous protruding stamens with reddish filaments and yellow anthers. Like many prairie plants, leadplant's central root system can extend 15' or more into the soil, enabling it to survive periodic prairie fires.

Habitat/Range: Occurs in numerous types of prairie habitats, hillsides, savannas, limestone glades, open woodlands, and along railroads and roadsides. Leadplant tolerates sandy, gravelly, or clay soils, and is an indicator of pristine or high-quality prairie habitat. Range is throughout most of the central Great Plains states, from New Mexico and Oklahoma in the west, north to Minnesota and the Dakotas, and east from Arkansas to northwest Indiana.

Uses: A pleasant tea can be made by steeping 1 tablespoon of dried leaves in 1–1½ cups of boiled water; the leaves may retain flavor after being steeped up to 3 times. The whole plant is used medicinally to treat a wide range of ailments, and leaves were used in smoking mixtures by some indigenous tribes. A showy attractant to pollinators, leadplant is a great addition to flower gardens and serves as a high-protein livestock and wild mammal forage.

Warnings/Comments: When western pioneers were first plowing the tough, pristine prairie sod, the long, stout leadplant roots would often break, making loud popping sounds like the breaking of string, earning it the name "prairie shoestrings." *A. fruiticosa* (indigo bush) has similar but larger leaf structures and purple spike flowers; it grows as a bushy shrub up to 12' tall. Its crushed fruits were used as a condiment, and stems of proper size were made into arrow shafts.

HOG PEANUT
Amphicarpaea bracteata

Edible parts/harvest time: Beans in mid- to late summer. Ground fruits and roots in fall to winter. Native.

Description: Hog peanut is an unusual plant because it produces two types of flowers and seeds. It grows as a trailing or climbing, often aggressive, vine up to 8'. Lacking tendrils, it climbs by coiling around adjacent stems or structures. Alternate leaves are trifoliate, occurring at intervals along the stem. Leaflets are broadly lanceolate to ovate, with smooth margins. The terminal leaflet is up to 2½" long, on a petiole, and is larger than the sessile lateral leaflets. Flower stalks form at intervals on the stem at leaf axils, with up to 12 flowers emerging on compact racemes up to 2" long. Flowers are ½" long, pale pink to lavender, each having 2 upright petals rolled at the edges, 2 slender lateral lobes, and a small keel. Flowers mature to flattened, curved pods up to 1½" long, each containing 3 or 4 mottled grayish beans. In addition, it produces inconspicuous belowground secondary flowers that mature to ½" or larger, round or pear-shaped fruits (peanuts) from the root stolons.

Habitat/Range: Occurs in moist prairies, woodlands, thickets, brushy ravines, and roadside banks in dry or moist soils. Range is the eastern half of Texas north to the eastern Dakotas

Hog peanut tubers and beans

and Minnesota, and throughout much of the eastern United States. Less common in the extreme southeastern states.

Uses: Hog peanut tubers are edible raw after hulling the brown skin but are better if cooked; they are a bit like a single-seeded peanut. Smaller rootlets can also be eaten. The small, aerial beans are edible, too, but should be cooked; they taste a bit like lentils.

Warnings/Comments: Wild beans should always be cooked before consuming in quantity. Hog peanut is common in suitable habitats and can be an aggressive colonizer in some conditions. The "peanuts" aren't always present but occasionally can be found in great quantity.

HOPNISS (AKA AMERICAN GROUNDNUT, POTATO BEAN, INDIAN POTATO)
Apios americana

FRITZFLOHRREYNOLDS, WIKIMEDIA COMMONS

Edible parts/harvest time: Beans in late summer to fall; tubers any time they are present. Native.

This plant's tasty tubers were heavily utilized by indigenous tribes, and the first European colonists were very fond of them. They have promise as a cultivated crop and probably would have been cultivated already if not for the somewhat time-consuming process to locate and dig the tubers and their long growth cycle.

Description: This perennial herbaceous vine has a 2-year growth cycle and grows to 10–20'. It lacks tendrils and climbs by entwining itself on other vegetation or structures. Hopniss is unusual among pod-bearing bean vines in this family in that its leaves are not trifoliate. It has alternate, compound leaves that are odd-pinnate with 3–9 leaflets, though 5 is typical. The leaflets are 1½–3½" long and ¾–2¼" across, with blades that are lanceolate, oblong-lanceolate, or ovate in shape, with smooth margins. The foliage exudes a milky latex when broken. Fragrant, showy flowers form in moderate to thick density on conical racemes; they are reddish brown to maroon or purple, with pealike wings and keel. Flowers mature to form cylindrical pods 2–4" long, each containing several maroon beans that turn brown with age. The shallow root system grows laterally and is fibrous, with rhizomes and tubers. The tubers are arranged at irregular intervals along the rhizomes like knotted ropes. Individual tubers are ½–3" long and ovoid to globoid in shape; the white interior is covered by a brown skin.

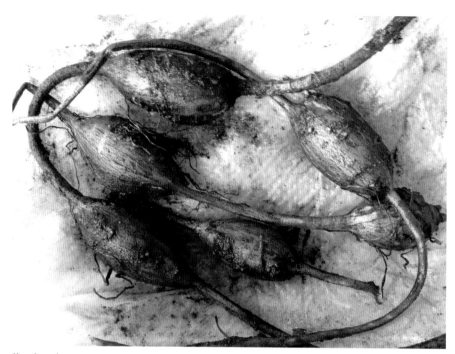

Hopniss tubers MALTE, WIKIMEDIA COMMONS

Habitat/Range: Prefers rich, moist habitats but may be found in dry areas. Occurs in moist to mesic prairies, woodlands, thickets, streambanks, sloughs, meadows, seeps, and edges of ponds, springs, and fens. Range is from Texas to South Dakota to the eastern half of the United States.

Uses: The tubers are an excellent food source with many health benefits and can be harvested any time of the year. They are sweetest when dug in late spring or early fall; second-year tubers get quite a bit larger but have tougher skins. Dig around the base of the vine to find the occasionally branching strings of rhizomes, then follow them to find the tubers. The tubers have a somewhat bitter latex and contain protease inhibitors that act as antinutrients, so they must be peeled and cooked to remove those. Young tubers can be peeled by rubbing with your fingers. Some recommend boiling the tubers first; they can then be fried, refried like frijoles, roasted, or added to cooked dishes. The shoots, flowers, and beans are also edible after cooking but best to leave shoots and flowers be, because the real food treasure is in the tubers. This is a beautiful flower garden addition and may be best suited to growing your own for consumption instead of harvesting from the wild in some areas.

Warnings/Comments: Some report a negative reaction to consuming the tubers, even after eating them for years with no effects. This could be from undercooking, but it's always best to try a small amount first to gauge your body's reaction. The beans contain up to 30 percent crude protein, the tubers about 17 percent. Both contain beneficial amino acids and are being studied in cancer research for their high levels of the anti-carcinogenic compound genistein.

MILKVETCH BUFFALO PEA (AKA GROUND PLUM)
Astragalus crassicarpus

ROCKY HOLLOW

Edible parts/harvest time: Ripe fruits in late spring and early summer. Native.

Description: A perennial with erect or sprawling hairy stems that form in small bunches up to 20", each bearing opposite compound leaves. Leaflets are up to ½" long and less than ¼" wide, elliptic, with a blunt or pointed tip. Several 3–4" flower stalks emerge from the leaf axils, producing up to 12 pealike flowers in terminal racemes. Individual flowers are about ¾" long with an erect, notched upper petal and 2 small, horizontal lower petals that are variably white, pink, lavender, or purplish in color. Smooth, light green fruits appear in early to late June. They are generally round or oblong, ½–1" long, with a central ridge, occasionally with a pointed tip, later ripening to pink or light purple. Each contains many small, black kidney-shaped seeds. As they mature, the heavy fruits often droop to the ground.

Habitat/Range: Found in prairie and glade habitats, fields, roadside embankments, ledges, bluffs tops, and rich and/or dry upland forest openings throughout most of the tallgrass prairie region. Its range encompasses prairie habitats and dry slopes in much of the Great Plains, from Montana to New Mexico and east from western Louisiana to Minnesota. Canada milkvetch (*A. canadensis*) somewhat resembles ground plum but has erect stems, larger leaves, and long, cream-yellow to green flowers that form in longer, more sparse racemes.

Uses: Eat the fruits raw on the spot, or slice and add them raw or cooked to any dish. They are a delicious addition to stir-fries and wild salads and can be pickled or lacto-fermented.

Buffalo pea fruits

Astragalus root has been used medicinally in other countries for centuries; ongoing studies confirm that the plant has many beneficial and medicinal properties.

Warnings/Comments: *Astragalus* is a large genus of over 3,000 species of herbs and small shrubs; it is the largest genus of plants in terms of described species. Some western species are called loco-weeds, as the leaves contain varying levels of the toxic glycoside swainsonine. Ingestion by livestock may cause locoism, a reaction that produces frantic, dazed, and uncoordinated behavior. No similar toxic species have fleshy, roundish fruits, but buffalo peas probably should not be consumed raw in large quantity. Canada milkvetch roots are reputed to be edible after cooking, but do not consume if a bitter taste remains, as it may indicate the presence of toxins. Unlike buffalo pea, its elongated green fruits are dry and inedible.

Lacto-fermented buffalo peas, before and after

RECIPE

LACTO-FERMENTED BUFFALO PEAS

3–4 cups buffalo peas, sliced in half, enough to mostly fill a quart jar

8–10 small bulbs wild garlic

Savory leaves such as fragrant sumac, horseweed, or other aromatics for flavoring

Optional: Small handful of gooseberries or buffalo currants, peeled curly dock or other tender shoots to fill up additional space in the jar. If you like spicy, toss in a small handful of peppercorns or a chili pepper or two. If available, a large wild grape leaf or other large nontoxic or non-bitter leaf is helpful to cover ingredients to keep them submerged. Commercial fermentation stones are available for this purpose.

Brine (roughly 1 tablespoon salt per 2 cups water heated in a pan till dissolved)

1. Clean a quart jar, lid, and band thoroughly with hot water and soap; rinse well. Rinse ingredients gently so as not to disturb the natural yeasts present. Add garlic bulbs to the jar first, then distribute other ingredients evenly, leaving about 1 inch of headspace. Cover with brine up to ½ inch from the top, then cover with a grape leaf or fermentation stone to keep ingredients submerged.

2. Tighten the lid but leave it loose enough for fermentation gasses to escape, then place in a shady spot. Alternately, the lid can be tightened fully, but it must be monitored and burped frequently to not build too much pressure. This method takes monitoring time and practice, and it's best to start with the first method. Fermentation should start at around day 4 or 5; contents will start to lose their bright colors, turning dull grayish green. Full fermentation is usually at 10–14 days; test by tightening the lid fully for a day or two. If the lid pops up with enough pressure to not push down easily, keep the lid loose for a few more days and test again; repeat until it doesn't build up pressure. Refrigerate and use within 3 months.

EASTERN REDBUD
Cercis canadensis

Edible parts/harvest time: Flowers in early spring. Leaves and seedpods in late spring and early summer. Native.

Redbud is a welcome harbinger of spring in prairie bottoms and adjacent woodlands. Its showy bursts of purplish-pink blossoms dot the brown hillsides just as the misty, pastel green of new leaf growth starts to appear.

Description: A small to medium-size understory tree 12–40' tall, usually with a crooked, branching trunk and spreading branches. Alternate, long-petioled leaves are 3–6" long, 2½–6" wide, orbicular to heart shaped, with a bluish-green, smooth upper surface, pale undersides, and smooth margins. Bark is gray to reddish brown and smooth on younger branches, developing shallow furrows and blocky scales with age. Twigs are smooth and brown, with white lenticels. Young shoots are olive green, often zigzagging with each leaf. Bloom clusters often cover the entire tree in late March–May before foliage emerges. Small buds on twigs and older branches produce umbellate clusters of 2–8 purple to rose-pink flowers on ¼" stalks. Individual flowers are 5 petaled, ¼–½" long, typical of those in the pea family. Flowers are replaced by abundant seedpod clusters. Individual

Redbud pods

pods look like miniature snow peas; they are green and leathery with tapered ends, 3–4" long, ½" wide, each containing 6–10 flattened, oval ¼" seeds. Pods will dry to brown and often persist into winter.

Habitat/Range: Occurs in in prairie potholes, sloughs and sinks, sandhill lakes, dolomite glades, rocky streambanks, bluffs, fencerows, and woodlands bordering prairies. Range is from Texas to southeast Nebraska, east to the coastal states. Absent from coastal areas of New England.

Uses: Raw flowers are a great trail nibble or addition to salads, and they make good jelly. Some people harvest them quickly by stripping large amounts of flowers off the twigs and branches, but this may also strip off the twig buds, inhibiting future blooms on that surface. When harvesting to retain the ornamental aspect, pluck the unopened buds and flowers by the stems without disturbing the twig buds. Young, tender leaves can be added to salad greens or cooked as potherbs. Young pods can be eaten raw, steamed, lacto-fermented, pickled, or added to stir-fries, soups, and other cooked dishes; treat them like miniature snow peas. They typically have a short window of edibility before becoming tough and fibrous.

Warnings/Comments: Flowers are reported to be high in vitamin C. Seedpods contain 25 percent protein, 8 percent fat, and 3 percent ash. A 2006 study determined that flowers and seeds are high in antioxidants and anthocyanins, as well as linoleic and alpha-linolenic acids. Often planted as an ornamental.

RECIPE

REDBUD FLOWER JELLY

This recipe works well with violet, spiderwort, wild rose, or any sweet and colorful flower petals.

1¾ cups redbud infusion

2 tablespoons fresh lemon juice

3½ cups sugar

⅛ teaspoon butter

1 pouch Certo fruit pectin

Infusion: Bring 2 cups water to a boil, remove from heat, add about 2 cups redbud flowers, and cover. Let sit for 10 minutes, then strain through layers of damp cheesecloth or a fine-mesh wire strainer.

1. Measure 1¾ cups (exact measurement) of prepared infusion into a 6- to 8-quart pot. Add lemon juice and sugar, plus ⅛ teaspoon butter to reduce foaming. Bring to a rolling boil on high heat while stirring. Stir in pectin and boil for 1 minute, stirring constantly.

2. Remove from heat and skim off any foam. Ladle quickly into prepared jars to within ¼ inch of the tops. Clean rims and threads, and fully tighten 2-piece lids. Allow to cool and then refrigerate. If storing unrefrigerated, boil jars and lids in a water bath before filling.

PURPLE PRAIRIE CLOVER
Dalea pupurea and others

Edible parts/harvest time: Leaves, stems, roots, and flower heads in late spring and summer. Native.

Description: An herbaceous perennial legume with 1 to several unbranched stems up to 3' tall growing from a common base. Flowers bloom from a cylindrical, spikelike terminal flowering head. Alternate leaves are odd-pinnate, finely cut in 3–5 divisions. Individual leaflets are opposite from the midrib, dark green, linear in shape, and about 1–2" long and ⅛" across. Blooms June–September, with pale magenta to rose-purple flowers forming terminally at stalk tips in tight, rounded to cylindrical heads 1–2" tall and half as much across. Individual florets have only 1 true petal about ¼" across, 4 petal-like modified stamens, and 5 golden anthers that protrude outward. The buds are covered by silvery hair, and flowers open in a circle around the base of the flower head, gradually moving upward.

White prairie clover (*D. candida*) is similar but has white flowers.

Habitat/Range: Grows in mesic to dry black-soil prairies, gravel or sand prairies, dunes, savannas, glades, rocky open woods, and along railroads and roadways. Range is throughout a large section of the central United States, from New Mexico to Mississippi, north from Montana to the Great lakes, and into Canada.

Uses: Young leaves and flower heads add nice flavor to salads and can be used to make tea. The stem can be peeled and eaten. The root can be eaten raw or cooked and is often chewed for its sweet and pleasant flavor. Used medicinally for numerous ailments; the bruised leaves can be used as a field-expedient poultice to treat wounds.

Warnings/Comments: Both species attract numerous pollinators and are unique additions to ornamental flower gardens. Due to their pioneering nature, deep-root stability, and nitrogen-fixing capabilities, they are used in revegetation efforts on disturbed or reclaimed land. Their root systems will often run 6 feet into the ground and spread through 18 cubic feet of soil. Both species are also high-protein livestock forage.

ILLINOIS BUNDLEFLOWER (AKA PRAIRIE MIMOSA)
Desmanthes illinoensis

Edible parts/harvest time: Green seedpods in late spring and early summer. Ripe seeds in mid- to late summer. Native.

Description: An herbaceous perennial 2–4' tall, unbranched or sparingly so, with mimosa-like leaves and globular flowers. The central stem is light green, grooved, and smooth to sparsely pubescent. Alternate, compound leaves are evenly bipinnate and up to 8" long with a fernlike appearance. Each compound leaf has 8–12 pairs of even-pinnate leaflets; each leaflet consists of 20–40 pairs of closely spaced subleaflets. Individual subleaflets are linear, about ⅛" long, light to medium green, ciliate along their margins, and mostly sessile. The rachises of the compound leaves are whitish green with fine hairs and grooved along their upper sides. Blooms June–July with globular flower heads about ½" in diameter, consisting of extremely tiny, 5-petaled white flowers (about 30–50 flowers per head) on axillary peduncles up to ⅓" long. Projecting yellow stamens give the flower heads a spherical, brushy appearance. Flower heads are replaced in late summer by tightly "bundled" green seed clusters up 1" across, eventually turning brown at maturity. These clusters contain about 5–15 curved and flattened seedpods, each about ½" long. Each

Illinois bundleflower seedpod

seedpod splits open to release 2–5 seeds; individual seeds are shiny reddish brown, flattened, and ovoid-reniform in shape.

Habitat/Range: Occurs in rocky or black-soil prairies, limestone glades, moist meadows, woodland openings, streambanks, ditches, waste areas, and along railroads and roadways. Most abundant in clay or sandy soils. Range is throughout the Great Plains states and much of the lower Midwest, east to Mississippi, and north to Illinois and Iowa.

Uses: Immature seedpods can be boiled as a vegetable when collected before they become tough. Seeds can be boiled or ground into flour. Flavor isn't exceptional (best when seasoned well or combined with other more flavorful species).

Warnings/Comments: Illinois bundleflower seed proteins are rich in sulfur-containing amino acids and appear to be greater or equal in protein to whole corn, wheat, and cooked oats. The protein in uncooked seeds was found to be 69 percent digestible, with digestibility rising to 83 percent after boiling for 30 minutes. It is noted as an important range plant due to its high protein content and is used in prairie restorations to improve dilapidated soil due to its nitrogen-fixing capabilities. Ongoing studies are considering large-scale production of bundleflower seeds for commercial human consumption.

AMERICAN LICORICE (AKA WILD LICORICE)
Glycyrrhiza lepidota

Edible parts/harvest time: Shoots and young leaves in spring. Roots are best in spring but can be harvested any time they are present. Native.

Description: An erect perennial with a coarse, hairy stem up to 3' tall and yellowish-white flower clusters that somewhat resemble large alfalfa flowers. Stems are covered with minute sticky hairs and can appear ridged. The spreading root system is rhizomatous and can be lateral or deep; individual roots may grow up to 5' or more. Alternate leaves are pinnately compound, with 11–19 lanceolate or oblong leaflets 1–1½" long and ½" wide. Individual leaflets have smooth margins, sharp tips, and glandular dots on their undersides. Flower clusters about 1–2" long form as terminal racemes on 1–2½" stalks arising from leaf axils. Individual flowers are cream or yellowish white, about ½" long, with 5 spreading or decurved petals. Structure is typical of those in the pea family, with one larger erect upper petal, two lower boat-shaped petals, and two lateral wings. Each flower is replaced by a dry, oblong green pod about ½" long, covered in hooked spines and containing several smooth greenish to brown seeds. The pods ripen to light then dark brown, and they persist into the winter.

Habitat/Range: Occurs in prairies, meadows, pastures, cultivated ground, waste areas, gravelly river bottoms, and along railroads and roadways. Often found in disturbed areas and tolerates clay, saline, or sandy soils. Range is throughout most of the western United States, east to the Texas panhandle, north through Iowa and Minnesota.

Uses: Young, tender roots can be eaten raw in the spring or cooked at later stages. They resemble sweet potatoes in flavor when roasted over an open fire. Lewis and Clark's expedition recorded preparation methods used by indigenous tribes: The root was roasted, then pounded to facilitate removal of the woody central "string," and the remainder was eaten like potatoes. The root is also used as a tea or beverage, and to flavor other foods. It can be chewed as a masticatory to cleanse the teeth and sweeten the breath, supposedly good for teething children. The root contains 6 percent glycyrrhizin, a substance that is 50 times sweeter than sugar. The tender young shoots can be eaten raw or cooked in the spring, until they get about a foot high. Used medicinally to treat a wide range of ailments, as is European licorice (*G. alba*). Field-expedient medicinal uses include chewing the root and retaining in the mouth to relieve toothache and crushing the leaves to use as a poultice on sores and wounds. Lewis and Clark gathered many plant specimens previously unknown to science, including this native species. They recorded finding wild licorice near the banks of the Missouri River on May 8, 1805.

Warnings/Comments: Young growth can reputedly be toxic to animals. As with any plant with strong, flavorful compounds, consume in moderation. Wild licorice has nitrogen-fixing capabilities and can be used as a pioneer species to revegetate bare or disturbed ground. It is often the first species to invade a receding alkali flat.

TIMPSILA (AKA BREADROOT, PRAIRIE TURNIP)
Pediomelum esculenta and others

Edible parts/harvest time: Roots in late spring to early summer. Native, found mostly in undisturbed prairies.

This once-common plant was a staple food for indigenous tribes of the central to northern Great Plains. Due to massive habitat loss, overgrazing, and fire suppression, it is now restricted mostly to pristine prairie remnants in protected preserves. The Lakota and other tribes still sustainably harvest this plant from healthy populations on tribal lands, but it shouldn't be collected in the wild unless found in abundance, and only then sparingly and with proper harvesting techniques. Best practice is to propagate and grow it in gardens, or to start and encourage new populations wherever suitable habitat exists. Seeds and starts are available commercially in many native wildflower nurseries.

Description: An erect, branched, and spreading perennial up to 18" tall with 1 to several stems emerging from a stout, thickened taproot. The entire plant is covered in dense whitish hairs. Alternate leaves are palmately compound on long petioles, each with around 5 leaflets arranged in a fan-shaped pattern. Leaflets are elliptic, 1–2" long and ½" wide, and densely hairy on the undersides. Blooms May–July with pale blue to purplish flowers forming in cylindrical terminal clusters up to 4" long. Individual flowers are around ½" long, with a flaring upper petal, 2 lateral petals, and a protruding split or keeled lower petal, typical of species in the pea family. Fruits are small and hairy beanlike pods. The sturdy brown

Braided timpsila tubers

roots form rounded, spindle-shaped tubers about 2–4" below the surface, each around 4" long. The fleshy tubers have a dark skin.

Tall-bread scurf pea (*P. cuspidatum*) is similar but with larger, smooth leaves, larger flower clusters, and a more southern range. Silvery scurf pea (*P. argophyllum*) has a distinctive pale silver appearance, smaller and sparser flower clusters, and its compound leaves usually have 3–5 leaflets.

Habitat/Range: Occurs in dry, rocky prairies and glades, calcareous hills, bluffs, open rocky woods, stream valleys, and open woodlands. Not commonly found outside undisturbed prairie habitats, timpsila is usually most prolific within quality habitats in protected remnants or preserves. Range is mostly prairie regions from Oklahoma to Montana, east to Minnesota, south to Arkansas.

Uses: The root is traditionally harvested at the end of the flowering stage. The main taproot is carefully excavated with the top connected, then the root is cut or twisted off, leaving a bit of it attached to the top. This is inserted upright back into a hole in the dug-up soil and packed down; the flower will continue to mature and drop seeds. This may give the seeds a higher chance of propagation than if deposited on undisturbed or compacted soils. The root must be peeled first and can be eaten raw but is much better when cooked by roasting, boiling, or frying. It can also be dried and ground into flour for immediate use or for storage, and used in soups, cakes, and breads. Peeled, dried roots were traditionally stored by braiding the small rootlets into ristras like chili peppers and garlic bulbs. Timpsila is more nutritious than most root crops, containing about 7 percent protein and over 50 percent carbohydrates, and is rich in trace minerals and vitamins, especially vitamin C (17.1 milligrams per 100 grams).

Warnings/Comments: The green tops are reputed to be toxic to livestock. For a more complete analysis of timpsila harvest, use, and conservation, I highly recommend Samuel Thayer's entry on this plant in his book *Incredible Wild Edibles*; he devotes 28 pages to it. There are numerous reasons for the plant's decline, but overharvest is not generally listed as a threat. Timpsila was a high-value food staple to indigenous plains people, as their winter meat-rich diet was often deficient in vitamin C. Oral histories suggest that their bison hunting camps were chosen based on proximity to large colonies of timpsila. They frequently sold and traded these and other wild plant foods to westward-bound pioneers, who were unaware that they had been driving over miles of these plants in their wagons. Several species are commercially available for use in edible/ornamental flower gardens.

WILD BEAN (AKA TRAILING FUZZY BEAN, AMBERIQUE BEAN)
Strophostyles helvola and others

Edible parts/harvest time: Beans in mid- to late summer and fall. Native.

Description: A robust trailing or climbing vine resembling a domestic bean but with fuzzy stems and fruits. Its trifoliate leaves are occasionally lobed, and it lacks the ground fruits of hog peanut. Individual flowers bloom only a few at a time and consist of an upright, flaring pink petal, 2 slender lateral petals, and a pronounced upright-curved keel. Flowers mature to clusters of cylindrical, fuzzy pods up to 3½" long, each containing several black, somewhat woolly-appearing cylindrical beans.

Sand bean (*S. leiosperma*) has similar flowers and fruits but is generally smaller with smaller, more lanceolate leaves, and its beans are smooth.

Habitat/Range: *S. helvola* occurs in tallgrass, mixed-grass, and sand prairie ravines, thickets, fencerows, sand and gravel bars, abandoned fields, floodplains, sandy and rocky woodlands, in or near croplands, and along streambanks and railroads. It tolerates a range of soils and conditions and can colonize disturbed ground. *S. leiosperma* occurs in similar habitats but is usually found in dry, sandy areas with sparse ground vegetation. Range of both species is from Texas through Nebraska to the Dakotas and Minnesota, and scattered locations throughout the central United States.

Uses: Harvest when young, then boil, steam, or add to cooked dishes like you would green beans. Ripe beans must be boiled to remove toxins.

Warnings/Comments: Dried beans may contain toxic lectins and should be cooked before consumption. Wild bean and hog peanut were both utilized by indigenous peoples; food remains have been found in archaeological excavations of prehistoric sites.

FAGACEAE (BEECHES, OAKS)

This family of deciduous or evergreen trees and shrubs comprises about 927 species in 8 genera and is characterized by alternate simple leaves with pinnate venation, unisexual flowers in the form of catkins, and fruit in the form of capped nuts.

BUR OAK
Quercus macrocarpa and others

Edible parts/harvest time: Nuts in fall. Native.

Acorns were among the most heavily utilized plant foods wherever they occurred by indigenous peoples. Processing was time-consuming, but the high protein/fat content and long storage life made them a dietary staple. Those willing to put in the processing time can produce their own tasty, gluten-free grain alternative.

Description: Oaks are split into two general groups, white and red. The white oak group is preferred because of lower tannin levels, but all can be used after processing. Leaves of the red oak group have small, sharp pins on the outer points, or lobes, of leaf margins. Leaves of the white oak group have rounded or pointed lobes, without pins. Bur oak has the largest acorns with the lowest tannin levels.

Habitat/Range: Bur oak occurs in bottomlands, black soil prairies, upland savannas, and dry sandy plains, where it prefers slopes of south and west exposure. In the western edge of its range, it is more abundant on moist north-facing slopes than on drier south-facing slopes. It is found throughout much of the prairie region of the Midwest. Other oak species are more commonly found in the easternmost parts of the central grasslands

Uses: After leaching, acorns can be used as any nut or made into a highly nutritious flour. First remove the caps and put the acorns in water; discard the floaters. Both cold water and hot water leaching methods can be used: Cold water is great to make flour and retains more nutrients; hot water is better for using broken bits as nuts.

Drying the acorns first makes it easier to remove the brown skin (testa) covering the nuts. Some say boiling them first helps with this and for removing the hull. Keep the peeled acorns in water until right before processing to prevent oxidization.

Grind the acorns to mush with a food processor or molcajete, then fill lidded quart jars one-third full or more and cover with water. Occasionally shake and let sit overnight. Every day, pour off the water through cheesecloth, then fill again with fresh water. Repeat this cycle for 5–8 days until the bitterness is gone. Alternatively, the mush can be placed into fine-mesh net bags and put into a stream of moving water for several days. Pour through double layers of cheesecloth (saving the nut milk) and squeeze all the liquid from the grit to make drying easier. Dry the grit without heat; once dried it can be used as flour or stored. The nut milk can be boiled to a one-third reduction then sweetened for drinking or used in soups or as a thickener. Salt-brine fermenting or dry-salt curing are other ways to remove tannins from whole acorns. These methods work well with red oak group acorns and others with higher levels of tannins as ways to preserve their higher fat content. Acorns can also be pressed to harvest the oil.

To use halves and bits as nuts, try hot leaching. Place pieces into a pot of boiling water till the water turns a tea color; repeat till water is mostly clear, usually 4–6 times or more. Always start with boiling water, as putting the acorns into water and then bringing it to a boil may set the bitter flavor. Roasting the bits afterward brings out flavor.

Warnings/Comments: Acorns must be leached before consuming, even those that aren't particularly bitter. They contain phytic and tannic acids; both act as antinutrients that bind with beneficial minerals and nutrients, preventing the gut from absorbing them.

GROSSULARICEAE (GOOSEBERRIES, CURRANTS)

This family has about 150 species of shrubs in two distinct groups: currants and gooseberries. They are native to temperate North America, extending southward into the Andes. Currants usually lack spines and have clustered flowers; gooseberries are usually prickly, with solitary flowers.

MISSOURI GOOSEBERRY, BUFFALO CURRANT

Ribes missouriense, R. aureum

Edible parts/harvest time: Berries in late spring and early summer. Native.

Description: A deciduous shrub up to 4' tall, usually round in shape with multiple thorny stems, occasionally forming large colonies. Older stems are gray to brown, erect to arching, prickly, with 1–3 larger spines at the leaf nodes. Young stems are green, hairy or prickly, occasionally smooth. Alternate leaves occur up the stems in bunches of 2–3 leaves. Each leaf is up to 2" across, generally orbicular, with 3–5 broadly toothed primary lobes that are rounded at the tips and wedge shaped at the base. White or pale green blooms appear in April–May, consisting of 2–3 small, drooping flowers emerging on short racemes at the leaf axils. Each flower consists of a narrow, tubular calyx and 4–5 narrow, often reflexed lobes, with 5 stamens that extend far out of the calyx. Fertilized flowers mature in early summer into round green berries up to ⅓" across, ripening to dark purple. Each contains numerous dark seeds.

Buffalo currant, aka golden or clove currant (*R. aureum*) is more commonly found in the western half of the United States. It has leaves similar to gooseberry but with lobes that are more deeply cleft and with fewer teeth at the margins, its stems lack spines, and its yellow flowers have a fragrant smell not unlike cloves. Fruits are golden yellow, orange red, brown, or black.

Buffalo currant

Habitat/Range: Gooseberries are found in scrubby prairies, pastures, thickets, old fields, glades, power line cuts, disturbed ground, and partially shaded fencerows. Range is the eastern two-thirds of Kansas and Nebraska, north into the eastern Dakotas, east to Lake Michigan, and south to Arkansas. Buffalo currant occurs in similar habitats from eastern Oklahoma north to the Dakotas, and over much of the western United States.

Uses: Green gooseberries are a tart, refreshing trail nibble, although some prefer them ripe and sweet. Ripe or green berries can be used in preserves, syrups, sauces, and juices and can be dried or frozen for later use. The tart flavor of green berries is preferred in pies, cobblers, and jam with the addition of a sugar or sweetener of choice. They are especially great for a burst of flavor when added to mixed lacto-ferments containing dock shoots, daylily buds, buffalo peas, etc. Buffalo currants have similar uses but tend to be sweeter.

Warnings/Comments: Some people report a dermatitis rash after touching gooseberry spines. All *Ribes* species are attractive natives suitable for edible landscaping.

JUGLANDACEAE (HICKORIES, WALNUTS)

Valued for both their wood and their nuts, this family consists of about 50 species of trees or shrubs in 10 genera. Persian Walnut (*Juglans regia*) is one of the major nut crops of the world and Black Walnut (*Juglans nigra*) is the most economically valuable tree in the Midwest.

PECANS AND HICKORIES
Carya illinoinensis and others

Pecan nuts, showing the 4-segmented hull typical of hickories and pecans

Edible parts/harvest time: Nuts in fall. Native. Southern pecan pie, hickory-smoked meat, ax handles, and longbows are examples of the usefulness of hickories. The nuts of several species are like pecans in flavor.

Description: Hickories are medium to large, straight-trunked trees, typically with short, stout limbs and a narrow crown. All have alternate, compound leaves that are odd-pinnate and 8–20" long. Leaflets are lanceolate to broadly ovate, 3–8" long, usually glossy, with serrated margins. There are 7 fairly common *Carya* species that form two groups. Pecan (*C. illinoinensis*) and bitternut (*C. cordiformus*) are members of the pecan hickories, with 7–17 leaflets and flattened, elongated terminal buds. Shagbark (*C. ovata*), shellbark (*C. laciniosa*), mockernut (*C. tomentosa*), pignut (*C. glabra*), and black hickory (*C. texana*) are members of the true hickories, with 5–7 leaflets and either small or large, egg-shaped terminal buds. A mature shagbark hickory is one of the easiest trees to identify by its bark, which peels from the tree in long, shaggy, often curved strips or plates.

Habitat/Range: Pecan is commonly found in riparian bottomlands, floodplains, savannas, streambanks, and forested habitats. Native to the eastern half of the United States, west to eastern Texas and the eastern half of Oklahoma, Kansas, and Minnesota. Other *Carya* species are found in the easternmost part of this book's covered range.

Uses: Use like any other nut. Pecans are the easiest to extract the nutmeats; other species can be time-consuming, as the shell chambers tend to be smaller or more convoluted than in other tree nuts. A nutpick or dental pick is helpful. First remove the husks; an easy way is to store them until they dry and open on their own. Put the nuts in a container of water and remove the bad ones that float. Boiling or baking the hulled nuts can make them easier to crack. An alternate processing method is to crack the shells thoroughly into small bits and

Shagbark hickory trunk, showing its namesake

cover with boiling water in a container. The shells sink and the nutmeats float, allowing them to be skimmed off the water's surface. Indigenous peoples made *pawcohiccora*, a hickory nut milk made by pulverizing the nuts shell and all, boiling the mush until thick and creamy, then filtering out the shells. Fire-roasting the nuts can give a nice smoky flavor. The cambium of many species makes a very strong wrapping or cordage fiber.

Warnings/Comments: Pecan, shagbark, shellbark, and mockernut are the tastiest hickories; other species can be bitter. Indigenous tribes left behind many "nutting stones," which were used to hold the nut in place while being cracked. A chert hammer-stone was used to peck a small depression into the flat surface of a piece of sandstone or other soft stone; some were pecked right into bedrock. An alternate method of cracking larger amounts is to spread them on a hard surface and use a brick or flat stone to crack several at once. Hammers are commonly used, but they often cause the nut to fly out.

RECIPE

SHAGBARK HICKORY BARK SYRUP

1 pound shagbark hickory bark pieces

Water

Sugar

1. Preheat oven to 350°F.

2. Rinse bark thoroughly in plain water (scrub if needed); discard pieces with lots of lichens on them. Spread the pieces on a flat pan and roast for 20–30 minutes. When finished roasting, bark should have a sweet-smoky aroma.

3. Put the pieces in a large pot and cover with water; bring to a boil then simmer for 30–40 minutes. Remove the bark and strain the liquid. Measure liquid, then return it to the pot. Add an equal amount of sugar and bring to a boil. Reduce heat to a simmer; cook until the volume is reduced by 25–30 percent, whisking to avoid scorching.

4. Cool; decant into bottles or jars.

BLACK WALNUT
Juglans nigra and others

Edible parts/harvest time: Nuts in fall. Native.

Description: Black walnut is a large, straight-trunked tree up to 100' tall with a rounded, open crown. Trunk bark is dark gray to nearly black with deep furrows; branch bark is grayish and smooth. Alternate, compound leaves are up to 2' long, odd-bipinnate with 11–23 leaflets, with a terminal leaflet often smaller than the side leaflets. Each leaflet is smooth, lanceolate or ovoid-lanceolate, up to 3" long and 1" across, with serrated margins. Flowers April–May, with male catkins and female florets on the same tree. Female flowers mature to green globoid nuts up to 2½" across, forming either singly or in pairs. The husks ripen to a splotchy yellow black and are wrinkled when they start to drop in September–October, eventually becoming black and mushy with staining oils. The woody, ridged nut inside has 4 interior chambers containing aromatic nutmeats.

Little walnut (*J. microcarpa*) is a smaller species found in west-central Oklahoma and parts of Texas and New Mexico.

Habitat/Range: Found in rich, well-drained soils, bottomlands, benches along streams, bases of bluffs, valleys, and mesic woodlands. Range is the eastern and midwestern United States and Canada, west to Texas, and north to the Dakotas. May be present or introduced in most western states.

Uses: Use them like any other nut, in salads, soups, sweet breads, ice cream, desserts, and other confections. To dehull large amounts, lay them in your driveway; vehicle tires will squish the hull and leave the hard nuts to be easily picked out. Or mash them with your foot and pick out the nut (gloves are handy to avoid staining your hands). Once they are hulled, cure/dry them for a couple weeks in a cool, dry place with ventilation. Afterward, they can be stored shelled or unshelled. Young unripe walnuts can be aged in alcohol to make nocino, an Italian black walnut liqueur. The hulls can be used to make dye for fabric or leather and have extensive medicinal properties.

Warnings/Comments: Hulls contain the compound juglone, which is toxic to fish and was used by indigenous tribes as a fish poison in still waters (now illegal). Its voluminous nut production for harvest and beautiful, dark heartwood make it the most economically valuable tree. The roots produce a compound that inhibits nearby growth, so it isn't compatible with nearby gardens. Fun fact: The Latin genus name *Juglans* translates to "Jupiter's nuts."

ITALIAN NOCINO

Large lidded jar

20 or so small green walnuts, gathered young enough to slice through with a knife

6 whole cloves

Optional flavorings: lemon zest, cinnamon sticks, vanilla bean, coffee beans. Wild flavorings could be fragrant or licorice bedstraw, lemon beebalm, fragrant sumac leaves, etc. (don't go crazy here, let the walnut flavor shine).

1 bottle (or enough to cover ingredients) vodka, moonshine, aquavit, or Everclear

Maple syrup, honey, or sweetener of your choice

1. Wash and halve the walnuts, using rubber gloves.

2. Add walnuts, cloves, and flavorings to jar and cover with alcohol.

3. Let sit in a cool, dark place to macerate for 30 days (aging in sunlight may produce sharper flavors).

4. Strain liquid into another container using a fine-mesh strainer to remove solids and sludge.

5. Sweeten to taste with equal parts water and sweetener. It is a liqueur and should be sweet, though some like it less so.

6. Place in tightly lidded bottles or jars for aging. It's best after about 6 months. The tannins and sharp flavors will mellow with time.

LAMIACEAE (MINTS)

This large, globally distributed family consists of about 7,000 species in 236 genera. Many species are cultivated for their fragrant leaves and attractive flowers, or for their medicinal properties. Mints characteristically have square stems and simple, opposite leaves, and many have two-lipped, open-mouthed tubular flowers. Some species have the aromatic mint smell, and some do not. Most are used as teas or flavorings; milder species are good salad ingredients.

LEMON BEE BALM
Monarda citriodora

Edible parts/harvest time: Leaves and flowers whenever they are present. Native.

Description: A showy annual or biennial about 1–2' tall, with unbranched or sparsely branched and pubescent 4-angled stems. Pairs of opposite leaves occur along the stem; upper leaves may be in whorls. Individual leaves are sparsely hairy, 1–3" long, ¼–¾" across, elliptic or elliptic-oblong in shape with a pointed tip, either sessile or tapering gradually to a short petiole. Margins are smooth to slightly toothed. Two to 6 rounded flower clusters form one atop the other on the flowering stalk. Individual flowers are about ¾" long, each consisting of a light pink to purplish-pink two-lipped corolla, two stamens and a pistil inside the corolla, and a 5-toothed tubular calyx that is green to purplish green. The upper lip of the corolla forms a protective hood, while the 3-lobed narrow lower lip functions as a landing pad for pollinators. Beneath each flower cluster is a whorl of white to pink to lavender narrow bracts. The crushed foliage has a pleasant lemon or oregano scent.

Habitat/Range: Occurs in rocky or sandy prairies, glades, pastures, open hillsides, and along roadways. Prefers alkaline soils and open grassland habitats. Range is throughout much of the southern half of the United States from Texas to Kansas, west to Arizona. Absent in Colorado.

Uses: Its citrusy flavor is excellent in teas, jellies, candies, food seasonings, and in cocktails like mint juleps and mojitos as an alternative to cultivated sweet mints. Leaves and flowers can be used sparingly in green salads.

Warnings/Comments: Lemon bee balm is a showy, useful plant that is a great addition to flower gardens but may grow excessively tall and topple over when grown in loose, rich soils.

WILD BERGAMOT (AKA BEEBALM, HORSEMINT)
Monarda fistulosa and others

Edible parts/harvest time: Leaves and flowers in spring and summer. Native.

Description: A tall, branched perennial up to 4' tall. Leaves are lanceolate to ovate, up to 4" long, with serrated margins. Flower heads up to 3" across form at the stem terminus; showy individual flowers are pink to pale lavender, about 1" long, tubular, with extended stamens and 3 drooping petals.

Habitat/Range: Found in prairies, savannahs, fields, roadsides, woodland borders, glades, and along roadsides. Range is most of the United States and southern Canada, absent in Florida and California.

Uses: Bergamot is great for food seasoning and teas. Add to black tea, roasted chickory/dandelion root tea, New Jersey tea, or persimmon leaf tea to make mock Earl Grey.

Warnings/Comments: A popular addition to flower and pollinator gardens; many cultivars are available in a wide variety of colors. I had wrongly assumed for years that the "oil of bergamot" listed as an ingredient in Earl Gray tea was from wild bergamot. It is actually from the peel of the bergamot orange (*Citrus bergamia*), a citrus fruit native to the Mediterranean.

FIELD MINT
Mentha arvense and others

Edible parts/harvest time: Leaves whenever present. Native, with introduced hybrids.
Description: Natives, introduced varieties, and hybrids of this perennial mint can be found in both hemispheres. It is an erect or sprawling herb up to 1½' tall, with leaves that are up to 2½" long, broadly lanceolate to ovate, with prominent veins and serrated margins. Whorled flower clusters appear above the leaf axils on the upper stem or at the stem terminus.
Habitat/Range: Occurs in rich, moist conditions along springs, in borders of marshes, fens, and lakes, wet prairies, and disturbed ground. Found throughout the United States, less common from Texas and Oklahoma east to North Carolina. Absent from Louisiana to South Carolina.
Uses: Hybrids and varieties of *Mentha* species are known for the classic mint, spearmint, and peppermint flavor found in teas, candies, jellies, and other minty delights such as the mint julep and mojito cocktails.
Warnings/Comments: The health benefits from consuming plants in the mint family are apparently not limited to humans and mammals. Studies have recorded an increase in growth performance and immune function when mint oils were included in the diets of Caspian whitefish and Caspian brown trout.

SLENDER MOUNTAIN MINT
Pycnanthemum tenuifolium

Edible parts/harvest time: Leaves and flowers whenever present. Native.

Description: An erect, many-branched, herbaceous perennial 2–3' tall with extremely narrow, almost needle-like sessile leaves and profuse terminal clusters of small, white flowers. Stems are hairless, with slender opposite leaves up to 3" long and ¼" across, each with a prominent central vein and smooth margins. The densely packed leaves on the stems give the plant a bushy appearance. All parts of the plant emit a strong, mint/oregano-like aroma when crushed.

Habitat/Range: Occurs in moist upland black-soil prairies and meadows, thickets, limestone glades, old fields, pastures, and along gravelly riverbanks and roadsides. Range is the eastern third of Texas, Oklahoma, and Kansas north to the southern half of Iowa and east to the coastal Atlantic states.

Uses: Slender mountain mint isn't as sweet as other mints but is still good as a seasoning for foods and for tea.

Warnings/Comments: Most wild mints are pollinator magnets and do well in flower gardens.

MALVACEAE (MALLOWS)

This family is composed of about 4,225 known species in 244 genera, including economically important species such as okra, cotton, cacao, hibiscus, and durian. Its members occur worldwide except in the coldest habitats but are most common in the tropics.

VELVETLEAF (AKA BUTTONWEED, INDIAN MALLOW, CHINESE JUTE)
Abutilon theophrasti

Edible parts/harvest time: Tender greens in late spring through summer. Seeds in late summer to early fall. Introduced, invasive.

Description: A weedy annual up to 7' tall, with sparsely branching stems and large heart-shaped leaves. Alternate leaves are on petioles up to 4" long; leaf blades are up to 8" long and across, cordate to orbicular-cordate, with slightly serrated margins and pointed tips. The primary veins of the leaves are palmately arranged. The entire plant is fuzzy to pubescent, with foliage that is mostly pale green with dull green upper surfaces. Blooms July–September, with single, short-lived flowers on short stalks developing from the axils of the upper leaves. Individual flowers are up to ¾" across, with 5 pale orangish to yellow petals, 5 pale green sepals, and numerous stamens with golden-yellow anthers surrounding the pistil in a cluster like other mallows. Each flower is replaced by a pale green, flat-topped fruit about ¾" across, turning dark brown at maturity. The fruit consists of a ring of about 10–15 flattened seedpods. Each seedpod has a stout beak and contains about 5–15 seeds. Seeds are initially white, quickly maturing to grayish brown, somewhat flattened, and either kidney or heart shaped.

Habitat/Range: Occurs in croplands (particularly corn and soybean fields), abandoned fields, vacant lots, waste areas, roadsides, construction sites, and along railroads and roadways. Prefers open, disturbed ground. Range is throughout the Midwest and eastern plains states to the East Coast, with scattered populations throughout the continental United States.

Uses: Velvetleaf is part of traditional Maldivian cuisine, known there as *maalbulha*. Young, tender leaves can be chopped and added to omelets, stir-fries, and other cooked dishes.

Velvetleaf pod and seeds

They are somewhat mucilaginous and slightly bitter when raw; freezing or cooking removes bitterness. Young seeds can be eaten raw, and older seeds can be leached, dried, and ground into flour.

Warnings/Comments: Due to the plant's invasive nature, take great care to avoid introducing viable seeds into new areas. Velvetleaf has been cultivated for fiber in China for over 2,000 years and has been anthropogenically distributed around the world for food and fiber. It is also an extremely competitive plant that steals light, nutrients, and water when introduced into agricultural crops, decreasing corn crop yield up to 34 percent. When destroyed, the plant releases a chemical odor into the soil that inhibits germination of crop seeds. Despite these drawbacks, velvetleaf is a good source of vitamins A, B6, and C, calcium, copper, folate, iron, manganese, magnesium, niacin, potassium, thiamin, and zinc. Its mucilaginous properties are said to be detoxifying agents as well as a rich source of soluble fiber.

RECIPE

MAS HUNI (MALDIVIAN BREAKFAST)

1 cup freshly grated or frozen coconut

1 cup finely chopped young velvetleaf leaves

2 (5-ounce) cans tuna packed in water, drained and flaked

2 green chili peppers, stemmed and minced

1 small red onion, minced

¼ lime, squeezed

Sea salt and freshly ground black pepper

Add ingredients to a bowl, toss with lime juice, season to taste, and serve with chapati flatbread or wild seed crackers (see Lamb's Quarter for recipe).

PURPLE POPPY MALLOW (AKA WINECUPS)
Callirhoe involucrate and others

Edible parts/harvest time: Greens and flowers in late spring to late summer. Roots in fall and spring during dormancy. Native.

Description: A sprawling, perennial wildflower with bright magenta cup-shaped flowers, often producing several vine-like stems up to 4' long from a large and fleshy taproot. Stems are light green to dull reddish purple and covered with spreading white hairs, usually upturned at the tips. Alternate leaves are on long, hairy petioles, up to 3½" long and 3½" across. They are generally orbicular in outline, with 3–5 deeply cleft, palmately divided lobes, often with secondary lobes at the leaf tips. Blooms May–August, with individual flowers on pedicels up to 6" long forming at the leaf axils. The flowers are about 1½–2½" across, consisting of 5 broad wine-red to purplish-red petals with white bases, a columnar reproductive structure, and a whitish-green to reddish-green calyx. The columnar structure expands outward slightly, revealing numerous white stamens and pinkish style branches. The flowers are replaced by flattened, reniform carpels arranged together like a ring, each containing a single seed.

Two other related edible species are commonly found in prairie habitats: Pale poppy mallow (*C. alcaeoides*) has weak, sprawling stems, white to pale pink flowers, and leaves that are narrowly lobed. Fringed poppy mallow (*C. digitata*) has erect, smooth stems with a bluish surface bloom and is 1–3' tall. Leaves are deeply lobed and slender, occurring mostly on the bottom half of the stem; flowers resemble those of purple poppy mallow but are more cup shaped. During a breeze, its bright magenta flowers atop nearly leafless green stems give the flowers an appearance of small wine cups dancing in the air.

Habitat/Range: Occurs in dry, open, disturbed areas, pastures, prairies, and roadsides. Readily grows in poor soil containing sand, gravel, or clay, but will grow taller in rich, loose soil. Range is Texas to Nebraska, west to New Mexico and Wyoming, with scattered isolated populations in Arkansas, Missouri, Illinois, and Iowa.

Uses: Roots are best when collected in late summer till spring when the plant is dormant; winter roots are sweetest. They can be roasted, boiled, or fried, and their mild flavor and slightly mucilaginous texture make them a good addition as a thickener to soups, stir-fries, and other dishes. They can also be sliced thin and dehydrated for later use. Young, tender leaves and flowers can be eaten as salad greens; older leaves develop hairs that make them more suitable for potherb greens or as a soup thickener. The small seeds can be eaten raw like the wheel-shaped fruits (cheeses) of common mallow.

Warnings/Comments: Leaves can resemble some toxic *Ranunculus* species, but those have leaves that are lobed all the way to the base, dull instead of glossy, and do not emerge from a fleshy taproot. Other species of poppy mallow are edible, but some species have limited ranges and may be endangered.

COMMON MALLOW
Malva neglecta

Edible parts/harvest time: Tender greens and flowers whenever present. Seeds in fall. Introduced.

Description: A low-growing annual with roundish leaves and multiple erect to prostrate stems that emerge from a taproot. Stems are usually vine-like with white hairs, up to 3' but usually smaller. Alternate, crinkled leaves appear on long petioles and are 2½" long and 3" wide or larger, orbicular to reniform, with a deeply indented base and 5–9 shallow lobes with wavy and crenate margins. Blooms April–October, with 1–4 flowers appearing on short peduncles above the leaf axils. Flowers are ¾" across, with 5 white, pink, or pale violet petals with pink longitudinal stripes. They emerge from a short 5-lobed calyx. The central reproductive column consists of a single pistil and numerous appressed stamens, typical of mallows. Flowers develop into button-like flattened discoid fruits, each with 12–15 seeds encircling the outer edge.

Habitat/Range: Found mostly in disturbed ground with moderate to rich soil, in gardens, croplands, barnyards, vacant lots, roadsides, and edges of yards and paths. Native to Europe, introduced throughout the United States and Canada.

Uses: Use young, tender leaves, flowers, chopped stems, and green seeds as a mild-flavored salad addition. All tender upper parts can be cooked as greens or added to soups and other cooked dishes. The green seeds can be pickled for use as capers. Like its relative okra, all parts of the plant develop a slight mucilaginous quality when cooked. After winnowing, mature seeds can be cooked like rice, roasted and added to seedcakes, or pickled and used as capers. Used medicinally to treat various ailments, the mucilaginous properties of mallow tea help relieve throat and stomach irritation.

Warnings/Comments: Fertilized, nitrogen-rich soil near croplands or in gardens may cause high nitrate concentrations in the leaves; avoid or consume only small quantities when collected in those conditions. In ancient Egypt, the root of marsh mallow (*Althea officinalis*) was boiled with honey to make a confection, which was the origin of our sugary, puffed gelatin treat by the same name.

MARTYNIACEAE (UNICORN PLANTS)

A family of 16 species in 4 genera, generally restricted to western or tropical America. They are characterized by having mucilaginous hairs that give the stems and leaves a slimy or clammy feel and fruits with hooks or horns. Some members of the genus *Proboscidea* are known as "unicorn plant" or "devil's claw" because of their horned seed capsules.

DEVIL'S CLAW (AKA UNICORN PLANT, RAM'S HORN)
Proboscidea louisianica and others

Edible parts/harvest time: Flowers, buds, and green seedpods in late June through early August. Seeds in August through early October. Native.

Description: An annual herbaceous plant 1–2' tall, with erect or decumbent spreading stems up to 3' long and clusters of showy flowers. Stems are thick and branched, with opposite leaves on 1–10" stout petioles that occasionally become alternate at the branch tips. Leaves are palmately lobed, heart to kidney shaped, up to 1' long and 8" wide, with wavy to smooth margins and rounded to pointed tips. The foliage is densely coated with glandular hairs carrying tiny oil droplets, making the plant feel oily to the touch with a strong odor. Flowers are borne on axillary or terminal racemes up to 12" long, each with 4–12 flowers. Blooms mid-July–August, often after summer rains. Each flower corolla is funnel shaped with 5 irregular lobes, 1–2" long, pinkish white to pale lavender in color with yellow-orange lines and purple or red spots inside the throat. Flowers mature to a dehiscent podlike seed capsule with a long, narrow, curving or hooked beak; the name "unicorn plant" refers to this feature. Each pod contains many ovate, flattened black seeds that are ½" long or longer. As the fruit dries and the flesh splits, the beak splits into two "claws" to facilitate seed dispersal as they hook onto the fetlocks of large ungulates and other animals. Each plant may produce up to 80 fruits.

P. parviflora and the yellow-flowered *P. althaeifolia* are similar species found in the Desert Southwest.

Devil's claw pods BENJAMIN GRABNER

Habitat/Range: Occurs in fields, croplands, overgrown pastures, feedlots, waste areas, and roadsides. Most abundant in disturbed ground and sandy soils. Range is east-central Texas, Oklahoma, and Kansas north to southern Nebraska, west to eastern New Mexico and Colorado. Also found in scattered or adventive locations in many eastern states, and in southern California.

Uses: The young, unripe seedpods can be eaten raw, boiled, steamed, fried like okra, or added to stews like Cajun gumbo. Roast and grind the pods to make gruel, porridge or a gluten-free flour. They are also great lacto-fermented or pickled; just use your favorite pickled okra recipe. When the pods start to get tough and turn darker in color, harvest the seeds. Buds and flowers can be mixed with other ingredients in salads and other dishes. The skins of the dried fruits were widely used in basketry by the Hopi, Apache, Havasupai, and Kawaiisu to form dark patterns in the weave. They were also used as sewing implements and a black dye can be made from them when mixed with ash. The Tohono O'odham domesticated the species, producing a larger, white-seeded variety that is grown ornamentally and cultivated for food like okra.

Warnings/Comments: Fruits may contain black or white seeds; white-seeded plants are more common in cultivation. The seeds have up to 43 percent oil content.

Dried pod with horns

MORACEAE (MULBERRIES)

This mostly tropical or subtropical family has over 1,100 species in 38 genera and includes other edible species such as fig, banyan, and breadfruit. A regionally local, related species is the native Osage orange, aka Bois d'Arc or hedgeapple (*Maclura pomifera*). Its large, green fruits have edible seeds, and its wood is the premier material for bowmakers.

RED MULBERRY
Morus rubra

ROCKY HOLLOW

Edible parts/harvest time: Leaves in spring. Fruits in June and July. Native.

Description: A fast-growing, small to medium-size tree up to 60' tall with a stout trunk and a rounded, branched crown. Trunk bark of larger trees is thin, grayish to brown, with shallow furrows and slight, flat ridges. Branch bark is brown, reddish brown, or gray, and smooth. Twigs have sparse lenticels with smooth, green shoots. Alternate leaves form abundantly on twigs and shoots; all bleed milky sap. Leaves are 3–6" long, up to 4" wide, simple with serrated margins, usually oval to ovate, but often with 3–5 moderate to deep lobes, a rounded base, and a pointed tip. Flowers appear in April–May and can be either dioecious or monoecious, with male catkins 2–3" long and female catkins 1" or less. Female catkins develop into cylindrical, aggregate fruits (resembling blackberries) up to 1¼" long that ripen to red or purplish black in late June–early August.

Habitat/Range: Occurs in floodplain valleys and woodlands, moist upland wooded slopes and their borders, fencerows, and glades; planted ornamentally in parks and yards. Range is the eastern half of Texas, most of Oklahoma and the eastern half of Kansas, to southeastern Nebraska. Also found in much of the eastern United States.

Uses: Mulberries are a great nutritious snack, packed with resveratrol, vitamins, and antioxidants. They can be used like any berry in pies, pastries, breads, muffins, sorbet, wine, syrup, and meat sauces. The berries deteriorate rapidly after harvest, so use quickly or dry or freeze for later use. Taste can vary among individual trees; some are better than others. Young, tender leaves can be mixed with other potherbs or dried for teas. The wood is good for making bows. The cambium layer of young shoots makes a strong cordage fiber. Parts of the plants are used medicinally to treat various conditions.

Warnings/Comments: The unripe fruits and mature leaves of *M. rubra* and other related species contain toxins that may cause a range of symptoms when eaten in excess, possibly causing mild euphoria, hallucinations, stomach distress, and diarrhea. White mulberry (*M. alba*) was cultivated 4,000 years ago in China and is now naturalized in the United States and across the globe as the preferred host plant for silkworm (*Bombyx mori*) production. Paper mulberry (*Broussonetia papyrifera*) is another invasive Asian species.

NELUMBONACEAE (LOTUSES)

Nelumbonaceae consists of a single genus with 2 species. American lotus occurs in North America; Sacred lotus (*N. nucifera*) occurs in Asia. Both species are rhizomatous aquatic plants that are rooted in soil in shallow, slow, or still water. Like water lilies, they have large, showy flowers and large, round leaves on long petioles that either float or are suspended above the water's surface.

AMERICAN LOTUS (AKA WATER CHINQUAPIN)
Nelumbo lutea

Edible parts/harvest time: Stem shoots and leaves in late spring. Seeds in early summer. Roots in August to late fall. Native.

Although cattails have earned the nickname "nature's supermarket," lotus could also claim the title with its sweet root, nutritious seeds, and vegetable-like leaves.

Description: A colony-forming, emergent-aquatic plant with large, concave-centered round leaves and showy yellow flowers. Rhizomes rooted in water-covered soil or mud produce long petioles, each connected to the center of a single bluish-green leaf with drooping wavy edges that is 1–2½' across. Young leaves float at the water surface; mature leaves are held 1–2' above the surface. Large, pale yellow flowers appear in July–September; each is up to 8" across, with 10–20 tepals, golden stamens, and a central yellow receptacle that matures to a flat-topped seedhead resembling a showerhead. It contains 10–20 round, hard-shelled and nutlike seeds encased in hollow chambers. The seedhead eventually turns brown and droops to release seeds into the water.

Habitat/Range: Prefers slow or still water with mud bottoms. Found in ponds, sloughs, oxbow lakes, shallow lake inlets, marshes, and wetlands with open water. Range is the eastern half of Texas to eastern Nebraska and scattered locations throughout the Midwest.

Uses: Freshly unfurled young leaves and stem shoots can be cooked like spinach; older leaves can be used to wrap other foods for baking. Harvest the nutritious seeds while still young and green by shelling and removing the small, bitter embryo. Eat raw or roasted, candied, cooked like peas, dried and ground into flour, or boiled and mashed as a cereal. The starchy banana-shaped tuber is harvested in the fall. The flavor is like sweet potato when baked and is popular in Asian-style stir-fries and soups. The hollow air chambers within the root give it a wagon-wheel appearance when sliced into rounds.

Warnings/Comments: An aggressive colonizer of ponds and waterways, lotus often chokes out other aquatic vegetation.

ONAGRACEAE (EVENING PRIMROSES)

This widespread family consists of about 650 species in 17 genera. It occurs on every continent except Antarctica, from boreal to tropical habitats. Many species have showy four-petaled flowers that are popular ornamental species, such as fuchsia.

SAND PRIMROSE (AKA EVENING STAR, SUNDROP)
Oenothera rhombipetala and others

Edible parts/harvest time: Shoots and leaves in spring. Flowers, buds, and seeds in July through October. Roots of first-year plants in fall after dormancy or new young plants in spring. Native.

Description: A night-blooming, erect and leafy biennial up to 6' tall with showy yellow flowers, often forming colonies. First-year growth emerges from a taproot as a basal rosette; basal leaves are lanceolate, with slightly dentate to serrate margins. Second-year flowering plants are variable, with 1 or more pale green to reddish central stalks, either branched or unbranched. Alternate leaves are densely packed on the stem, with smaller secondary leaves often forming at the leaf axil. Each primary leaf is up to 7" long and 2" wide, lanceolate, sessile, or on short petioles, with smooth to slightly dentate margins. Blooms June–October, with flower clusters forming on racemes at the stem apex and branch terminus. Each flower is roughly 1" across, with 4 yellow diamond-shaped petals, several protruding stamens, and a long green calyx. Seed capsules are long and thin, containing numerous tiny brown seeds that are wind dispersed.

The Midwest is home to around 22 species of *Oenothera*; several are planted ornamentally, and all are edible. Common evening primrose (*O. biennis*) is similar to sand primrose but has rounded flower petals. Missouri evening primrose (*O. macrocarpa*) is a low-growing glade and prairie resident with large yellow flowers. The pink-flowering showy primrose (*O. speciosa*) may be common on roadsides.

Habitat/Range: Found in prairies, pastures, old fields, glades, bluff openings, gardens, roadsides, power line cuts, cropland borders, old fields, and edges of upland or bottomland forests. Range is throughout the United States and Canada, more common in the eastern half of the United States. Absent from Idaho, Wyoming, Colorado, Utah, and Arizona.

Uses: The sweet flowers, flower buds, and young basal rosette leaves can be eaten raw in salads or added to cooked dishes. Flower stalk leaves are best as a boiled potherb. Young shoots of the flowering stalk can be peeled and eaten raw or cooked. First-year roots can be gathered all year but are best in spring. They can be peppery when eaten raw but are milder when boiled or cooked, and they can be added to boiled potatoes or other milder vegetables. Some say they resemble parsnips in flavor and are a good candidate for pickling. There seems to be a lot of regional variability in flavor. If the roots are too pungent for your taste, grind the cooked root and mix with a bit of water, vinegar, and salt to use as a horseradish-flavored condiment. Young seedpods are edible and have numerous uses. After roasting or baking, they can be used like sesame or poppy seeds. They can be baked in breads, sprinkled into salads and soups, used with other wild seed mixes for ingredients in pickles and lacto-ferments, or steamed and added to other vegetables for a tasty side dish. All parts of the plant have been used medicinally for numerous ailments. The dried flower stalk makes a good hand drill for friction fire.

Warnings/Comments: Some people report minor throat irritation when consuming the plant, even when cooked; sample a small taste and wait a bit to check your body's reaction. *O. biennis* has been naturalized in temperate climates around the world and is commercially cultivated to make medicinally beneficial evening primrose oil.

OROBANCHACEAE (BROOMRAPES)

Comprising annual or perennial herbs and shrubs, and mostly parasitic plants of the order Lamiales, with about 2,000 species in 90 genera.

LOUSEWORT (AKA WOOD BETONY)
Pedicularis canadensis

Edible parts/harvest time: Leaves and flowers as soon as they emerge until they become tough. Native.

Description: This perennial semi-parasitic plant has showy flower clusters on unbranched, hairy stems up to ½–1' tall. The foliage primarily consists of a basal rosette with leaves up to 6" long and 2" across. Leaves are lanceolate or oblanceolate, with angular pinnate lobes and crenate, undulating margins. Except for being thicker and heavier, they have an almost fernlike appearance. Flowers appear as a spiral when viewed from above, forming on a conical, ragged spike atop each stem. Individual flowers are yellow to brownish purple, about ¾" long, and tubular with two lips. The upper lip curves downward and forms a protective hood, and the lower lip acts as a landing pad for pollinators. Flowers bloom from the bottom up during late spring, with a flowering period of around 3 weeks.

Habitat/Range: Occurs in moist or dry open prairies, open woodlands, savannas, thickets, bottomlands, and around lakes and streams. Prefers sandy or acidic soils. Range is eastern Texas to the eastern Dakotas, and much of the eastern United States.

Uses: Young leaves and fresh flower heads have a somewhat strong flavor and can be added to salads or cooked as a vegetable. The plant has a long history of internal and external medicinal use and was prized by Native Americans for its muscle-relaxing and possible aphrodisiac qualities.

Warnings/Comments: Due to its ability to parasitize potentially toxic plant roots, avoid consuming in large quantities.

OXILIDACEAE (WOOD SORRELS, SHAMROCKS)

A small family of trees, shrubs, and herbaceous plants consisting of 570 species in 5 genera. Most species are herbaceous with five-petaled flowers and have divided leaves that exhibit "sleep movement," closing at night. The genus *Averrhoa* contains the tree species that produces star fruit.

VIOLET AND YELLOW WOOD SORREL (AKA SOURGRASS, WILD SHAMROCK, SHEEPSHOWERS)
Oxalis violacea, O. stricta

Edible parts/harvest time: Leaves, flowers, and seeds whenever present, mostly spring and fall. Native.

Description: Violet wood sorrel (*O. violacea*) is a low-growing perennial that emerges from bulbs, with flowers that are typically taller than the leaves. Leaves are trifoliate, up to 1" across, in clusters on single stalks up to 6". Heart-shaped leaflets are dark green, with dark purple markings and purple undersides. The 5-petaled flowers are lavender to pale magenta, ¼–½" across, on umbels at the top of stalks up to 8" tall. The flowers mature to small, inconspicuous, egg-shaped fruits.

Yellow wood sorrel (*O. stricta*) forms erect, many-branched, weak, and often hairy stems up to 15" tall. Leaves resemble *O. violacea* but are light green and often larger. Small yellow flowers occur in small umbels at the leaf axils. Fruits (pickles) are upright, elongated capsules containing tiny black seeds. The capsules can expel the seeds a short distance when touched.

Habitat/Range: Violet wood sorrel is found in partial to well-shaded areas, prairies, rocky open woodlands, glades, and wooded roadsides, mostly in acidic soils. Yellow wood sorrel is widespread and tolerant of a wide range of conditions, occurring in open fields and edges, urban lawns and lots, waste areas, gardens, and other disturbed ground areas. Both species range throughout most of North America, absent from a few western states.

Uses: Raw leaves and seeds make a good trail nibble or a tasty addition to salads or sandwiches. When paired with peppergrass (*Lepidium* spp.), it adds a nice lemon-pepper flavor to any dish. Can be added to soups or other cooked dishes to add flavor or steeped to make a tart beverage. One wild table event I participated in featured wood sorrel ice cream—you'd have sworn it was lemon flavored!

Warnings/Comments: The genus name *Oxalis* refers to this plant's high oxalic acid content. All plants containing higher levels can cause stomach distress and other conditions if consumed in excess. The houseplant purple shamrock (*Oxalis triangularis*) is a South American relative of wood sorrel that has the same characteristic lemony flavor.

RECIPE

CREAMED WOOD SORREL SOUP

3 tablespoons butter

½ cup finely chopped wild onion or shallots

4½ cups vegetable stock or seasoned water from boiled greens

½ cup marsala wine

6 packed cups chopped violet or yellow wood sorrel leaves

½ cup heavy cream

Salt

1. Melt butter in a stockpot. Add onions and sauté till tender; add the vegetable stock and wine. Turn the heat to medium.

2. Stir in the sorrel leaves and cook a couple minutes till the leaves are wilted. Reduce heat, cover, and cook another 10 minutes, stirring occasionally.

3. Whisk in the cream; salt to taste and let simmer on very low heat for about 5 minutes.

4. Serve garnished with chopped wild onion tops and fresh sorrel leaves and flowers.

PHYTOLACCACEAE (POKEWEEDS)

This family's taxonomic status is still under debate; different sources report a range of 33 species in 5 genera to 65 species in 18 genera. Most are trees, shrubs, and herbaceous plants with tropical or subtropical origins; several are found in temperate climates. Many have common characteristics, such as simple leaves with entire margins and fleshy, racemose fruits.

POKEWEED (AKA POKE SALLET)
Phytolacca americana

My first memory of foraging was collecting pokeweed with my mom; it was always served with bacon grease. It is one of the tastiest cooked greens when it is harvested at the proper time and prepared correctly. It is often called "poke salad," but the actual term is "sallet," referring to cooked greens. (See "Warnings/Comments" on why to never use it raw in a salad.)

Edible parts/harvest time: Shoots and top leaves in early to mid-spring. Consume only after boiling or cooking! Berries (juice only) in late summer to fall. Native.

Description: A large, pithy-hollow branching stem up to 10' tall with smooth, pale green skin, maturing to bright purple. Alternate, light green leaves are lanceolate to ovate, up to 10" long and 4" wide, with smooth margins and prominent veins on ½–1" petioles. Small white flowers form in cylindrical clusters on 3–6" terminal racemes and mature to drooping clusters of dark purple, juicy berries. Each is about ¼" across, containing 10 small, oval black seeds.

Habitat/Range: This native, disturbed-ground colonizer can be found in barn lots, pastures, old fields, damp meadows, edges of bottomlands and moist forested slopes, fencerows, power line cuts, roadsides, bases and ledges of bluffs, streambanks, and pond and lake edges. Range is throughout the eastern United States and Canada, west to Texas, Oklahoma, Kansas, and southeastern Nebraska. It is adventive in the western coastal states and Arizona, absent from the Dakotas to Idaho and from Nevada to Colorado.

Uses: Must be cooked before consuming! Young shoots up to 8" tall and tender tops of young plants under 1' tall are considered the most delicious of potherbs after boiling to remove toxins. Some sources advise boiling in 3 waters, but this is unnecessary. Small

Pokeberries

shoots and top leaves of young plants require only a single good boil till the water turns greenish. With plants up to a couple feet tall, take only the tender topmost leaves and stem, and blanch before boiling. The berry juice is great for syrup, jelly, and wine, but only after straining out the toxic seeds. They are small, so use a fine-mesh strainer or cheesecloth. The juice also makes a nice purple dye, but a mordant must be added to make it colorfast. Cherokee and other indigenous peoples used a specific dosage of dried seeds to relieve arthritis pain. The roots have been used medicinally, but only by those who have studied the subject extensively. Using toxic plants for medicine is all about dosage; mistakes can range from unpleasant to fatal.

Warnings/Comments: When trying pokeweed for the first time, boil well in at least 2 waters and eat only a small quantity to check your body's reaction. When harvesting shoots, take care to avoid any pieces of taproot. The toxin levels increase as the plant gets larger, so avoid collecting when the stalks start turning purple. The toxic berries can be attractive to toddlers; remove them if you have little ones about. Consumption of even a few berries could be fatal at that age. In early foraging experiments, I tried steaming the leaves instead of boiling. The result was quite explosive, probably akin to eating a whole box of Ex-Lax. Lesson learned: always boil them!

PLANTAGINACEAE (PLANTAINS)

This herbaceous family has been recently reclassified and is now considered to include about 1,900 species in 94 genera worldwide in various structural forms, with 247 species in 52 genera found in the United States. All are herbs with predominantly undivided basal leaves and flowers produced in elongated or branched clusters.

BROAD-LEAVED PLANTAIN (AKA COMMON PLANTAIN, WHITE MAN'S FOOT)
Plantago major and others

Edible parts/harvest time: Leaves whenever present and tender. Seeds in midsummer to fall. Introduced.

Description: This well-known European invader forms a basal rosette with large, oval, shiny and leathery leaves up to 12" long, each with 5–9 prominent lateral veins and smooth margins, tapering to a long petiole. When broken, the petiole contains stringlike threads that continue into the leaf veins. Flower spikes grow up to 15" from the base, forming inconspicuous flowers on the upper two-thirds of their length that mature to densely packed fruit capsules, each containing 6–20 brown seeds.

Narrow-leaved plantain (*P. lanceolata*) has narrower, less fleshy, lanceolate leaves with a cone-shaped flower atop a long, naked stalk. The Midwest hosts several native plantain species.

Habitat/Range: Found throughout the United States and southern Canada in moist, disturbed ground and open areas, especially lawns, fields, urban/suburban waste areas, and roadsides nearer to human habitation. Tolerates a high degree of disturbances like trampling and mowing. Native to Europe and Asia, naturalized in many other countries around the globe.

Uses: Young leaves are a highly nutritious addition to salads or can be blanched, sautéed, or soaked in water overnight to improve flavor. Larger leaves can be used in soups or boiled with other greens as a potherb before they become tough. Seeds can be consumed raw, boiled like rice, or dried and ground for use as a flour additive or in seedcakes. The leaves are used raw as a poultice or made into an ointment to treat wounds, stings, rashes, and other skin ailments. Tea from the leaves is used to treat bronchitis, colds, sinus infections, and stomach ulcers.

Warnings/Comments: Plantain may cause contact dermatitis, diarrhea, and blood-pressure drop when eaten in excess, though reports of these are rare. It is one of the most widely distributed and commonly used edible/medicinal plants in the world. Studies confirm that broad-leaved plantain is vitamin rich and contains bioactive compounds and antimicrobial properties for use in treating numerous ailments and conditions. Not related to cultivated cooking bananas (*Musa* spp.), also called plantains.

POLYGONACEAE (BUCKWHEATS, KNOTWEEDS, DOCKS, SMARTWEEDS)

This weedy family includes rhubarb and buckwheat and contains about 1,200 species distributed into about 48 genera. Polygonum is derived from ancient Greek. *Poly* (many) and *gonum* (joints or knees) refers to the characteristic swollen nodes on the stems of many species.

CLIMBING BUCKWHEAT (AKA CRESTED BUCKWHEAT)
Fallopia scandens and others

Edible parts/harvest time: Leaves, stems, flowers and seeds in early summer to fall. Native.

Description: An aggressive climbing vine, this perennial can form large, twining mats on trees, shrubs, and structures. Stems are round, have swollen nodes with an attached membranous sheath at the leaf axils, and are light green to red and up to 20' long. Alternate leaves are ovate to heart shaped, up to 6" long and 3" wide, with smooth margins. Lower leaves are on long petioles; upper leaves are nearly sessile. Blooms appear July–November, with large clusters of yellow-green to pinkish, minute flowers forming on racemes at leaf axils along stems. Flower is a 5-parted calyx with 3 outer tepals that are strongly winged. Three-angled, winged fruits approximately ⅓" long mature to contain smooth, shiny, brownish to black tri-cornered seeds, typical of other buckwheats.

Black bindweed (*F. convulvus*) is similar with similar uses, but its flowers and fruits are keeled instead of conspicuously winged, and the sides of its 3-angled achenes are dull instead of shiny. It is a fast-growing, introduced annual that can become invasive in croplands.

Habitat/Range: Found in moist, mostly open areas in bottoms, valleys, glades, streambanks, edges of impounded waters, sloughs, and seeps, ledges and tops of bluffs, croplands, fencerows, ditches, railroads, and roadsides. Range is throughout eastern North America and Canada, west to Texas, Colorado, and Wyoming.

Uses: Tender young leaves and stems can be eaten raw as a salad green, cooked as a potherb, added to other cooked dishes, or blended with sweetened water for a tart drink. Older stems can be cut up and used like rhubarb. Seeds can be eaten raw, dried for use in seedcakes, or ground with other seeds as a flour substitute.

Warnings/Comments: Those prone to kidney stones or gout should avoid plants with high levels of oxalates. Toxic species in the genus *Convulvus* (bindweeds related to morning glory) have large, trumpet-like flowers and milky sap, and lack the swollen nodes with membranous sheaths (ocrea).

SMARTWEEDS
Persicaria spp.

Water smartweed

Edible parts/harvest time: Shoots, leaves, and flower heads whenever present. Native and introduced.

Description: Erect-stemmed perennials found in dense colonies, usually in moist or disturbed ground. Stems are 2–5' tall, slightly zigzagged, with swollen nodes at the bends at leaf axils, and a papery sheath (ocrea) around the stem at the node. Alternate leaves are on short petioles or sessile, mostly lanceolate, with smooth margins and sharp tips, up to 6" long but usually smaller. Most species feature spikelike, cylindrical flower clusters up to 6" long that occur at the tips of stems. Individual flowers are pink or white, up to ⅛" across.

There are over 15 species of *Persicaria* in the Midwest, all with somewhat similar characteristics. Pink smartweed (*P. bicornis)* is up to 6' tall with showy pink flowers and slender green leaves. Water smartweed (*P. amphibia*) is up to 3' tall with pink flowers and larger shiny leaves, and is found in or near water. Dotted smartweed (*P. punctata*) is similar but with sparse, white flowers. Nodding smartweed (*P. lapathafolium*) is tall with drooping white or pink flower spikes and often has a dark chevron on the young leaves. Lady's thumb (*P. maculosa*) is a pink-flowered garden invader from Eurasia. Jumpseed (*P. virginiana*) has larger, broader leaves and a flower spike up to 16" with sparse, small white flowers. The oval, podlike dried seeds will jump off the stem when touched.

Nodding smartweed

Habitat/Range: Found in prairie ravines, seeps, wet ditches, gravel bars, waste areas, gardens, lawns, and borders of lakes, ponds, streams, and sloughs. Many species can live submerged in water or soggy ground. *P. amphibia*, *P lapathafolium*, *P. maculosa*, and several others occur throughout much of the United states. *P. bicornis* is found in the central plains states. *P. virginiana* and *P. pensylvanica* are found in the midwest and throughout the east.

Uses: A nibble-and-spit test helps for smartweeds; some species are mild, some are tart, and a few are uncomfortably hot and bitey. The young, tender leaves and flower heads of milder species are a good addition to green salads. Young shoots can be boiled as a potherb or added to cooked dishes such as stir-fries, soups, and quiche. Some species have a very peppery flavor and are best used sparingly or as a seasoning.

Warnings/Comments: A British nickname for this plant is "arse smart," as some species such as water pepper (*P. hydropiper*) contain high levels of caustic oils that can cause skin irritation (presumably named from people popping a squat and the plant contacting a bare bum). A milder form is cultivated in Japan for culinary purposes.

FIELD SORREL (AKA SOUR DOCK, RED SORREL, SHEEP SORREL)
Rumex acetosella

Field sorrel leaves

Edible parts/harvest time: Leaves, shoots, flowers, and seeds whenever present. Introduced.

Description: A low-growing herbaceous perennial that first emerges as a basal rosette up to 6" across, with a slender, erect flowering stalk up to 1' tall but usually shorter. It spreads by rhizomes and often forms colonies. Basal leaves are up to 3" long and 1" across, spear shaped and narrowing at the base, with 2 spreading basal lobes. Blade surface is smooth, with smooth margins. Tiny brownish-red flowers form in racemes on branched, green to reddish flower stalks.

Habitat/Range: Prefers mostly open or disturbed ground habitats. Found in prairies, glades, gardens, lawns, pastures, old fields, and along paths and roadsides. Native to Europe; range is throughout North America and Canada.

Field sorrel flowers

Uses: Vitamin-packed, nutrient-dense, and loaded with healthful phenolic compounds, the leaves and young stems are great as a lemony-tasting trail nibble or tart addition to raw salads. Use in sauces, soups, and other cooked dishes when a sour or tart element is desired. Can be dried and ground into flour as a thickener or used to make noodles. Seeds can be eaten raw or cooked. Used medicinally as a diuretic and for other ailments, and topically for its astringent properties.

Warnings/Comments: Consume only small quantities of raw plants, as overconsumption may cause stomach distress or aggravate kidney stones. Cooking may reduce oxalates to negligible amounts.

CURLY DOCK (AKA YELLOW DOCK)
Rumex crispus and others

Edible parts/harvest time: Leaves, shoots, and stalks as soon as they emerge. Seeds in late summer and fall. Introduced and native.

This highly nutritious potherb was another of my mom's favorite wild greens, usually boiled with pokeweed and served with the ever-present bacon grease and vinegar. I was an adult before I knew boiled greens and most cooked vegetables had a flavor other than bacon.

Description: First-year growth is a small basal rosette of dark green, oval to lanceolate leaves that mature to 6" long and 1" across with pointed ends. Young leaves have smooth margins, becoming crisped and wavy with age. A distinguishing feature is the papery sheath (ocrea) that forms on the leaf stem as it emerges from the root or stalk. Second-year plants form a ridged flower stalk up to 4' tall, with alternate leaves along the stalk, usually branching as it flowers. Clusters of green flowers appear on panicles of racemes at the ends of stems and branches, maturing to reddish-brown clusters of papery-husked, 3-angled brown seeds. The dried flower stalks and seed clusters often persist into winter.

Broad-leaved dock (*R. obtusifolius*) is similar with broader leaves and margins that are less curled. The native species pale dock (*R. latissimus*) has paler, softer leaves.

Habitat/Range: Found in open, disturbed ground in a range of soil conditions. Common in pastures, old fields, glades, garden edges, roadsides, degraded wetlands, cultivated fields, and waste areas. Native to Eurasia; range is throughout the United States and Canada.

Curly dock basal leaves with (inset) seedhead

Pale dock

Uses: Young, tender leaves and shoots can be sparingly used raw in salads. Shoots, leaves, and larger peeled stalks are usually boiled as a potherb or used in soups, but harvest while they still have a slight mucilaginous texture and before they become dry and tough. Long, tender leaves of some *Rumex* species are used to make aveluk for a traditional Armenian soup of the same name. Whole fresh leaves and young stems can be pickled or lacto-fermented. For the latter, leaves should be rolled up tightly, put into a quart jar with shoots or peeled stems, then covered with a brine solution of roughly 1 tablespoon salt per 2 cups water. Use a fermentation stone to keep ingredients submerged to avoid mold. Let sit for several days till a sour pickle flavor is achieved, then refrigerate. Leaves and shoots can be blanched or sautéed and frozen for later use. Seeds can be winnowed, ground, and used as a flour additive, or ground with other seeds such as lamb's quarter and climbing false buckwheat mixed with wheat flour to make tasty crackers. For quick relief of temporary itching from contact with stinging or wood nettles, crush a few moist leaves of dock or jewelweed (*Impatiens capensis*) and scrub the affected area.

Warnings/Comments: People with liver or kidney dysfunction, kidney stones, or rheumatoid arthritis should avoid plants in this family. Consuming large quantities of raw leaves may result in stomach distress.

RECIPE

ARMENIAN AVELUK FOR SOUP BASE

Select the longest fresh basal leaves, twist and braid them into long braids, and dry them in a cool, well-ventilated dry area. Leaves gathered after the flowering stem is up may be more bitter. The traditional braids were up to 4 times the height of the person making them.

The long drying time allows lacto-fermentation to take place, giving the leaves a different aromatic flavor and texture, reminiscent of cured tobacco. The braids are cut into lengths for soup stock and combined with other ingredients such as lentils, potatoes, leeks, plums, etc. There are many recipes available, including salads and traditional Armenian aveluk soup.

RECIPE

CURLY DOCK NORI

4 cups chopped curly dock leaves (or mix with lamb's quarter or any flavorful seasonal greens)

5 cloves garlic

1 tablespoon chopped peppergrass tops/white smartweed leaves (or 1 teaspoon black pepper)

1 teaspoon soy sauce

1 teaspoon water

1. Blend all ingredients to a paste in a food processor or blender. Add water if needed; the mixture should be thick like tomato paste.

2. Lay parchment paper on a flat dehydrator tray or baking sheet. Spread paste in a thin layer on the parchment paper; dehydrate at 125°F for about 12 hours, or until crunchy. Alternately, bake at 200°F till the mixture starts to dry; flip mixture and turn off the oven to prevent burning. Remove when cooled and paste is dried to a crunchy texture; break into chip-sized pieces

3. Use the nori as you would chips, or crumble over the top of soups and other dishes.

PORTULACACEAE (PURSLANES)

This family consists of mostly fleshy-leaved herbaceous plants or shrubs in a single genus with about 115 species. The highest diversity occurs in semiarid regions of the Southern Hemisphere in Africa, Australia, and South America. A few species extend north into temperate and Arctic regions.

SPRING BEAUTY (AKA FAIRY SPUD)
Claytonia virginica

Edible parts/harvest time: Leaves and flowers in spring. Tubers whenever present. Native.

This beautiful perennial has delicate, white flowers with pink stripes and can be found in blooming carpets with other early-spring ephemerals. Any plant that produces something called "fairy spuds" is a winner in my book; the brown-skinned root corms resemble tiny potatoes.

Description: One to several narrow, lanceolate leaves 2–5" long that are dark green to purplish in color emerge from a small corm. The weak flowering stem usually has 1 or 2 sets of opposite leaves, terminating in a raceme of 3–6 flowers. Flowers are up to ½" wide, with 5 white, pink-striped petals and 5 central stamens with pink anthers. The root is a round white corm with brown skin and attached rootlets up to ½".

Habitat/Range: Occurs in a range of habitats; found in moist prairies and woodlands, hollows, bottoms, rocky ledges, along shaded streams and in urban lawns. Range is the eastern third of Texas, Oklahoma, and Kansas to Iowa, and in most of mid- to eastern North America.

Uses: All aerial parts are a tasty addition to salad greens; the leaves have a slight citrus-sweet flavor. The flowers add a nice bit of color and sweetness. The tubers can be harvested any time but are best when collected in late winter or early spring as the leaves are forming. They can be eaten raw or cooked; their flavor is like potatoes but sweeter.

Warnings/Comments: Use caution when collecting to make sure the tubers are fairy spuds and not the larger corms of jack-in-the-pulpit (*Arisaema triphyllum*). It and other plants in the Arum family contain sliver-like calcium oxalate crystals (raphides) that can embed themselves into soft tissue in the mouth.

PURSLANE
Portulaca oleracea

Edible parts/harvest time: Leaves, stems, and seeds in early summer through fall, any time it is present. Introduced.

Purslane is currently receiving much attention due to its superfood status. It has the highest levels of plant-based omega-3 fatty acids and is packed with beneficial vitamins and minerals.

Description: Reddish, succulent stems radiate from a central taproot, typically prostrate and sprawling but occasionally upright. It often forms dense mats. The thick, fleshy leaves are up to 1¼" long, spatulate, smooth with smooth margins, alternate or opposite, clustered at stem joints and ends. Small, yellow, 5-petaled flowers form singly on leaf axils, maturing to form small seedpods containing numerous tiny, black seeds.

Habitat/Range: This disturbed-ground invader tolerates a wide variety of soil conditions and is drought tolerant. Found in open habitats such as fields, barnyards, gardens, croplands, rocky bluffs, gravel roadsides, abandoned urban lots, and cracks in sidewalks. Its original range was possibly India and Persia, but it is now found nearly worldwide due to anthropogenic distribution.

Uses: Leaves and stems are used raw in salads and make a nice addition to just about any raw or cooked dish. The taste is a citrusy tang with a slight pepper finish and goes well with nearly anything. Its slightly mucilaginous quality makes it a good addition to soups and stir-fries and also a great base for pesto. The tart taste is due to malic and oxalic acids. As with many plants growing in desert or dry environments, it has more flavor when harvested in the morning. The seeds can be added to other ground seeds and ingredients to make nutritious seedcakes.

Warnings/Comments: Common in vacant city lots and sidewalks where toxins may be present. Plants are easily transplanted or grown from seed. Purslane is increasingly available in farmers' markets and health food stores due to its nice flavor and numerous health benefits. It was originally thought to be of Eurasian origin, but recent archaeological evidence shows that it was used by indigenous peoples in pre-Columbian North America.

RECIPE

WILD PESTO

I prefer a mix of both mild and sharp flavors. Mild flavors can be anything with moist or fleshy leaves, such as purslane, lamb's quarter, violet leaves, chickweed, pink smartweed, etc. Plants with sharper flavors include horseweed, wild bergamot or other mints, white smartweed, peppergrass, and watercress.

3 cups purslane and/or fresh mixed greens

4–5 bulbs wild onion (or 4–6 cloves garlic)

¼–½ cup choice of seeds or nuts

½ cup freshly grated Parmesan

Splash of lemon juice or small bunch of wood sorrel leaves

¼ cup extra virgin olive oil

Salt and pepper to taste

Crush first 5 ingredients together in a molcajete, or put in a food processor. Add olive oil a bit at a time to preferred viscosity; season with salt and pepper to taste.

RHAMNACEAE (BUCKTHORNS)

Rhamnaceae is a large family of flowering plants—mostly trees, shrubs, and some vines—commonly called the buckthorn family and included in the order Rosales. The family contains about 950 species in 55 genera.

NEW JERSEY TEA
Ceanothus americanus

Edible parts/harvest time: Leaves and flowers in late spring and summer. Native.

Description: A shrubby deciduous perennial up to 3' tall, with 1 to several erect stems that terminate with aromatic flower clusters. Stems emerge from a stout taproot that can grow to depths of 15'. Stems are light green to light yellow, pubescent to hairy, becoming woody with age. Leaves are mostly alternate, occurring along the entire length of each stem. Individual leaves are up to 3" long and 2" across, oblong to ovate, with finely serrated margins. The upper leaf surface is often rough or wrinkled along these veins. Blooms May–June, with upper stems terminating in panicles of white flowers on long peduncles; axillary panicles also develop from the axils of upper leaves. Individual panicles are 2–5" long and 2–3" across with lateral spreading branches up to 1½" long. Flowers are replaced by small 3-lobed seed capsules, becoming dark brown or black at maturity. Each capsule contains 3 glossy brown ovoid seeds; the capsules later split to expel the seeds up to several feet.

Prairie redroot or narrow-leaved New Jersey tea (*C. herbaceus*) has larger leaves that are more sparsely arranged on the stems. Its flowers are on roundish panicles up to 4" across, with individual ¼" flowers on long, moderately dense to open pedicels.

Habitat/Range: Occurs in rocky tallgrass and mixed-grass prairies, glades, thickets, and open woodlands. Range is the eastern half of Texas, Oklahoma, Kansas, southeastern Nebraska and Minnesota, eastward throughout the eastern United States.

Uses: Primarily used green or dried as a tea, with a flavor resembling imported black tea when cured properly. Leaves can be combined with those of wild bergamot (*Monarda* spp.) to make mock Earl Grey tea. *Ceanothus* species contain no caffeine. The flowers are rich in saponins and can be used to make a mild soap. The plant is best harvested when in full bloom.

Warnings/Comments: New Jersey tea was widely used as tea and medicine by indigenous tribes. It was also quite popular as a replacement for imported black and green tea during the American Revolutionary War.

ROSACEAE (ROSES, APPLES, NUMEROUS FRUITS AND BERRIES)

A family of herbs, shrubs, and trees consisting of about 4,828 known species in 91 genera. It contains many important food species, such as apples, pears, plums, cherries, apricots, almonds, blackberries, and strawberries, and ornamental shrubs such as roses and hawthorns.

SERVICEBERRY (AKA JUNEBERRY, SARVUS, SHADBUSH)
Amelanchier arborea and others

Edible parts/harvest time: Flowers in early spring. Berries in June and early July. Native.

Description: A shrub or tree up to 35' tall, often multi-stemmed. Young limbs have smooth, often mottled gray bark that becomes ridged and furrowed with age, especially at the base of larger trunks. Simple, light green leaves are 2–5" long, alternate, ovate with a pointed tip, with finely serrated margins. Young shoots and leaves are covered in downy hair, becoming less so as they mature. Blooms appear in mid-March–late April before the foliage appears. Flowers have 5 wavy, long and narrow white petals that are slightly spaced, forming on 4–7" racemes at the tips of shoots in drooping clusters of 6–14 flowers. Flowering racemes mature in mid-June, forming clusters of fruits. Individual berries are round, ¼–½", ripening to dark red or purple.

Saskatoon berry (*A. alnifolia*) is similar but is usually a shrub or small tree less than 18' tall, with leaves that are nearly orbicular.

Habitat/Range: Occurs in limestone glades, steep or rocky slopes, along streambanks, above bluffs, and in open woodlands. Range is the eastern half of Oklahoma and southeast Kansas, north to the Great Lakes region, and over much of the Midwest and eastern United States. Saskatoon berry occurs in northern Nebraska, north to the Dakotas and Minnesota, and in the western United States. Both have a short window of availability.

Uses: Great for topping cereal or desserts and can be added to muffins, pancakes, bread, soups, etc. Makes excellent jam and wine. Dried serviceberries

Saskatoon berry

were a preferred addition to pemmican, a dried meat-and-berry travel food used by indigenous tribes. One preparation method uses a skinned and eviscerated rabbit or squirrel carcass that is dried whole then pounded to a fine mush and mixed with rendered fat and a handful of dried berries. This can be stuffed into a length of smoked deer intestine, much like a sausage. The rendered fat acts as a preservative, the sought-after fatty marrow inside the pulverized bones is retained, and the dried berries provide vitamin C to make it a complete food.

Warnings/Comments: Commonly planted as an attractive ornamental shrub, with several cultivars available. The berries attract wildlife, and leaves are very colorful in the fall. The blooms are an important nectar source for early-emerging pollinators.

HAWTHORN
Crataegus mollis and others

Edible parts/harvest time: Flowers, leaves, and buds in early to late spring. Berries in early to midsummer. Native.

Description: A shrub or small tree with single or multiple trunks and crooked branches, often forms a rounded crown. Trunk bark is gray brown and shallowly furrowed with scaly plates. Branches are gray and generally smooth, usually with sparse, woody spines. Twig bark is brownish with white lenticels. Alternate, simple leaves are 3–5" long and 2–4" across, forming on hairy petioles that emerge from twigs and shoots. Leaf blades are variably oval, spatulate, or triangulate, with pointed or serrated lobes along the margins. Blooms April–June, with clusters of white flowers forming on twig spurs. Individual flowers are up to 1" across, each having 5 petals and numerous yellow stamens. Fertile flowers are replaced by ½"-long reddish fruits resembling crabapples, each containing numerous small seeds.

Habitat/Range: Occurs in a variety of habitats such as rocky hillsides, glades, savannas, abandoned pastures, streambanks, thickets, and woodlands and their borders. Some species are more often associated with bottomlands. Range is the eastern third of Texas, Oklahoma, Kansas, and Nebraska to southern Minnesota. At least 7 *Crataegus* species occur in the central grasslands.

Uses: Process by cooking ripe fruits in a bit of water, then harvest pulp by squeezing through cheesecloth or a fine-mesh strainer to remove seeds. The pulp is delicious when used in jellies, sauces, syrups, wines, teas, and other beverages. Perfectly ripe fruits contain a high amount of pectin; pulp can be added to other fruit jellies when commercial pectin isn't available. Tender young leaves, flower buds, and flowers can be eaten as a trail nibble or added to salads. Hawthorn is known for its heart-health benefits and was used for centuries by ancient Druids, Greek and Chinese herbalists, and other cultures. It is commercially available as a supplement.

Warnings/Comments: Raw seeds should not be consumed in quantity. They contain the toxin amygdalin, an almond-scented hydrogen cyanide precursor found in the seeds of apples and many other related fruits. It can be harmful if consumed in quantity when metabolized after the seeds are crushed or chewed. Prairie crabapple (*Malus ioensis*) has similar fruits and growth structure but with generally narrower leaves and showier flowers. Its fruits are edible, but some varieties are too bitter for consumption.

RECIPE

HAWTHORN BERRY KETCHUP (A TRADITIONAL BRITISH CONDIMENT)

3½ cups hawthorn berries (or substitute other similar berries like silverberry)

1½ cups water

1½ cups cider vinegar

¾ cup sugar

½ teaspoon salt

Freshly ground black pepper

1. Remove stalks and wash berries, then put in a large pan with the water and vinegar. Bring to a boil, reduce heat, and simmer for 15 minutes or until the skins break.

2. Break up berries with a flat potato masher, then pour and work into a wire strainer placed over a pan to remove seeds and skins.

3. Add sugar and cook on low heat, stirring often. Simmer for up to 10 minutes, reducing the liquid to the desired consistency.

4. Salt and pepper to taste, then transfer to clean, sterile bottles. Store for up to a year.

WILD STRAWBERRY
Fragaria virginiana

WALTER SIEGMUND, WIKIMEDIA COMMONS

Edible parts/harvest time: Leaves in early spring. Berries in May and June. Native.

Encountering a large patch of ripe wild strawberries is the ultimate in flavorful foraging. Just remember to leave a few for the box turtles and other critters!

Description: A low-growing herbaceous perennial up to 6" tall, spreading by horizontal runners. Trifoliate basal leaves are on long, hairy stems. Each leaflet is ovate to obovate, up to 2½" long and 1½" wide, with toothed margins and hairy undersides. Blooms April–May, with umbel-like clusters of 4–6 flowers on long, hairy stalks. Flowers are up to ¾" across, with 5 rounded white petals and many central yellow stamens. Fertile flowers mature in June–July to red, fleshy aggregate fruits up to ½" across, with tiny seeds in sunken pits across the entire surface.

Mock or Indian strawberry (*Duchesnea indica*) is a similar, weedy nonnative with yellow flowers instead of white. The berries are white-fleshed and tasteless but nutritious.

Habitat/Range: Found in prairies, open woodlands and their borders, old fields, glades, rocky hillsides, savannas, and along roadsides. Tolerates a wide range of open and partly shaded conditions; occurs in disturbed or pristine habitats. Range is throughout the United States and Canada except for shortgrass prairie and desert habitats.

Uses: Great as a trail nibble. If you're lucky enough to find a large patch, collect and use as you would any berry, or use your imagination to make new concoctions. Best used fresh; the flavor is superior to the larger domesticated varieties. Green or fully dried leaves make good tea. The leaves and fruit are used medicinally to treat various ailments.

Warnings/Comments: Our common domesticated strawberry was first cultivated in eighteenth-century France and is a hybrid between *F. virginiana* and *F. chiloensis*, a South American species.

WHITE AVENS (AKA CLOVE ROOT, CHOCOLATE ROOT)
Geum canadense

RANDY A. NONENMACHER, WIKIMEDIA COMMONS

Edible parts/harvest time: Tender basal leaves in spring. Roots for beverages in early spring and late fall. Native.

Toxic look-alikes: Thimbleweed, see "Warnings/Comments."

Description: An herbaceous perennial with pubescent, branching round stems, mostly trifoliate leaves, and terminal small white flowers. The plant first emerges from a shallow taproot with a ball of small rootlets, forming a distinctive low, dark green basal rosette up to 6" across. Dark green leaves are on long petioles, odd-pinnate and/or roundish or palmate in shape with shallowly lobed and scalloped margins. The basal rosette leaves are completely different from the cauline leaves. A flowering stem emerges up to 1½' tall, with alternate cauline leaves that are mostly trifoliate or raggedly cleft on short petioles at the lower half, and simple, alternate leaves on the upper half that are mostly sessile. The leaf blades are up to 4" long and 3" wide, becoming smaller as they ascend the stem. The uppermost leaves look like a smaller single leaf with 2 little wings. Prominent veins give both basal and cauline leaves a wrinkly appearance; the veins appear to be incised into the leaf. Leaf margins are roughly serrate or cleft. Blooms May–October, with flowers about ½" across consisting of 5 bright white petals, 5 triangular green sepals about the same length, and 10 or more stamens surrounding a cluster of green carpels with elongated styles. Flowers mature to a green, spheroid, burr-like cluster about ¾" across, consisting of achenes with dried styles that are hooked at their tips, eventually turning brown.

Habitat/Range: Occurs in thickets, brushy fencerows, moist valleys or swales, along power line cuts, roadsides, yard edges, and borders of streams and ponds, in open woodlands and their borders, and tallgrass prairies. Range is from central Texas to the eastern Dakotas, east from Maine to northern Georgia.

Uses: The tender leaves can be used in salads or as a potherb, but they are better when mixed with other greens. The real treat is the clove-chocolate flavor when making tea with the roasted roots. The root is a small, fleshy nub with a ball of small, spreading rootlets attached. The size of the basal rosette doesn't always reflect the size of the root, so collect the roots with the largest root balls and replant those that are too small to yield much mass.

Warnings/Comments: The mildly toxic thimbleweed (*Anemone virginiana*) may appear somewhat similar but doesn't have the distinctive odd-pinnate basal leaves. It also has 1–3 flower stalks with a single 5-petaled flower at the top of each tall stalk; the petals are pointed instead of rounded. Consuming the plant would cause problems only if eaten in quantity. Making 1 cup of white avens chocolate beverage takes quite a few root clusters, so collect only when found in abundance and replant the smaller ones.

White avens fall rosette, with (inset) spring rosette

RECIPE

WHITE AVENS HOT CLOVE/CHOCOLATE

6–8 white avens root nubs and rootlets per 2–3 cups water

1. Chop up the nubs and rootlets.

2. Roast them in the oven or a skillet on the stovetop till they reach a golden-brown color. Some suggest breaking off the rootlets and using only the nubs, but I've used both and it turned out fine. The roast is critical: not enough and it won't have the flavor; too much and it will taste burnt.

3. After roasting, simmer in a pan with 2–3 cups water for 10–15 minutes.

4. Add sweetener to taste if desired (I use a bit of honey or stevia). Add cream for the full ride, and serve hot.

WILD PLUMS AND CHERRIES
Prunus americana and others

American plum

Sand plum

Edible parts/harvest time: Fruits in July to early September. Native.

At least a dozen *Prunus* species are found in the central grasslands; all are edible and delicious when properly prepared.

Description: American plum is a multi-stemmed, thicket-forming shrub or small tree up to 20' tall. Trunk of some species can be up to 12" diameter, with rough, gray to reddish-brown bark. Smaller stems are mostly smooth with lateral lenticels. Growth pattern of thicket stems can be twiggy and contorted, often with short spines. Alternate, simple leaves are ovate to obovate, 2½–4" long, 1½–2" wide, with pale undersides and sharply serrated margins. Blooms appear in April–May before foliage is present, forming at leaf axils in clusters of 2–5 flowers. Each flower is on a short stalk, with 5 white petals, 5 greenish sepals, and numerous stamens, up to 1" across. Fertilized flowers mature into globe-shaped yellowish to red fruits up to 1" across, with juicy, sweet/tart flesh when fully ripe. Each fruit contains a round and slightly flattened pit.

Sand plum (*P. angustifolia*) is similar but with narrower leaves and redder, shinier fruits; it is more commonly found in Kansas, Oklahoma, and scattered locations in Texas. Its range extends throughout the Midwest to the East Coast. Chokecherry (*P. virginiana*) has growth structure and foliage somewhat resembling wild plums but generally has smaller, dark red to purplish fruits and doesn't occur in the southeastern United States. Western sandcherry (*P. pumila*) is an easily overlooked deciduous shrub around 2½' tall, but may grow to 6' depending on the variety. It often forms dense clonal colonies by runners emerging from the root system. Branches may be upright or prostrate, spreading to ascending from low, sprawling basal stems about ¾" in diameter. Alternate leaves are 1½–2½" long and up to 1" wide, narrowly elliptic to oblanceolate, leathery, with finely serrated margins. It has the largest fruits of all wild cherries and is mostly restricted to sand prairie habitats. Wild black cherry (*P. serotina*) grows as a large tree up to 60' tall, with rough, scaly bark and shiny black racemose fruits that are globoid and ¼" across.

Sand cherry

Black cherry

Habitat/Range: Found in a wide range of habitats: glades, savannas, thickets, fencerows, abandoned pastures, ravines, streambanks, roadsides, power line cuts, and open mesic woodlands and their borders. Plums may colonize disturbed, open ground, but they are often shaded out by larger canopy species. Range is throughout most of the United States and eastern Canada.

Uses: All wild plums and cherries are great as a trail nibble, but they make the best jam or jelly ever slapped on a biscuit. Also good for pies, fruit salads, fruit leather, wine, brandy, sauces, or syrup, they can be dried or frozen for later use. Flavor varies widely among individual plants, from sweet to extremely tart. The sour astringent flavor turns sweeter when dried or cooked. Process by putting fruits in a saucepan, then add enough water to barely cover them. Simmer until the flesh can be worked off the seeds, then strain through jelly cloth if making jelly, or a wire strainer if making syrup, jam, or fruit leather. I prefer to use less heat (not quite a simmer) to preserve the vitamin C. The Lakota and other indigenous people make *wojape* (fruit stew) with chokecherries for use as a dessert or fry bread topping, or as a sauce with roasted meat and/or vegetables. Some indigenous peoples consider the seeds of larger *Prunus* species to be as important as the fruits. The seeds are hulled and the nuts inside leached to remove the amygdaline toxins.

Chokecherry

Warnings/Comments: Leaves, twigs, and pits of most species in the genus *Prunus* (cherries, peaches, and plums) contain the compound amygdaline, which breaks down into hydrogen cyanide when ingested. Wild plum is the source for numerous cultivar species that are sold commercially.

WOJAPE SAUCE

Alan Bergo's excellent food blog *The Forager Chef* has a great article on this dish. Traditionally it was made by pulverizing the whole fresh fruits, pits and all, into flat cakes, then dried cracker dry. These cakes were added to water, then cooked and thickened into a stew. His unique twist was to use timpsila (prairie turnip) flour as a thickener.

6 cups ripe chokecherries (substitute or combine with any wild fruit or berry such as buffalo currant, wild plum, sandcherry, blackberry, huckleberry, etc.)

1–1½ cups water

Maple syrup or honey

1. Slow-simmer fruits in water for 10–15 minutes or until flesh comes off the pits easily. Remove pits (if left in too long they can leave a bitter flavor). Simmer and reduce the remaining flesh until a jam or thick syrup consistency is achieved.

2. Sweeten to taste with maple syrup or honey. Some fruits may be fine without added sweetener, while some will be quite astringent and require sweetener to offset the tartness.

3. While sauce is still hot, place in sterilized lidded jars; it will keep for a couple months when refrigerated.

PRAIRIE ROSE
Rosa arkansana and others

Edible parts/harvest time: Flowers in late spring through summer. Hips in late fall, sweetest after first frost. Native.

Description: Prairie rose is a deep-rooted and long-lived shrub, usually under 3' tall; its underground rhizomes often form large colonies. Young stems are green, maturing to red, spreading to ascending, and covered in slender, stiff spines of variable size. They may die back every several years due to drought or freezing and are replaced by new shoots. Alternate leaves are 3–5" long, stalked, odd-pinnately compound, with 7–11 leaflets. Leaflets are up to 1¼" long and ¾" wide, obovate to elliptic, with coarsely serrated margins. Leaf stalks are up to 1" long, hairy, with wing-like appendages (stipules) at the base. Blooms midsummer, with 1–4 very fragrant flowers forming at tips of new shoots and occasionally at tips of second-year lateral branches of older, woody stems. Flowers are on smooth stalks, up to 2" across with 5 broad, rounded petals with wavy edges, often notched at the tip. Colors range

from nearly pure white to deep rose pink and are often bi-colored, with numerous yellow stamens in the center. Flowers mature in the fall to fruits (hips) that are around ½" across, each containing several small and fuzzy brownish seeds. Hips may persist into winter.

Several *Rosa* species occur in the central grasslands. The introduced invasive multiflora rose (*R. multiflora*) is a much larger, thorny shrub with numerous small, white flowers; its ripe hips are quite sweet.

Habitat/Range: Occurs in dry or sandy upland prairies, hill prairies and bluffs, limestone glades, pastures, thickets, fencerows, abandoned fields, open woodlands, and along railroads and roadsides. Range is a large swath of the northern two-thirds of the United States, from New Mexico east to Missouri, and north from Montana to the Great Lakes region.

Uses: The fleshy exterior of the hips has an apple-like flavor and can be eaten raw or processed into many useful foods or flavoring items. Deseeded hips can be candied, stewed, made into syrups and jellies, or dried for storage and used for flavorings, soups, or added to other cooked dishes or desserts. Flower buds and very young shoots are edible; flower petals can be eaten fresh, made into flower jelly, or used to make rosewater. Dried leaves can be used for tea. The stems of some species make serviceable arrow shafts, and fiber from the bark was used in making cordage. The entire plant is used medicinally.

Warnings/Comments: There are no toxic *Rosa* species, although some plants that have "rose" in the name are not true roses. Some sources state that 3 or 4 hips may contain as much vitamin C, calcium, phosphorus, and iron as an orange or lemon. The dried fruits often persist into winter, which made them a critical food source for indigenous peoples in scarce times.

COMMON BLACKBERRY
Rubus allegheniensis and others

Edible parts/harvest time: Flowers and leaves for tea in spring. Fruits in late June and July. Native.

Many folks engage in the midsummer ritual of berry picking. It's always worth battling ticks, chiggers, and brambles in the heat of summer when heavenly cobblers and pies are the result. Despite the name, these are aggregate fruits, not true berries.

Description: Common blackberry is an erect, spreading bramble with arching canes up to 8' tall. First-year canes and new growth on older canes are green and prickly, becoming ridged and brown with numerous decurved thorns with age. Compound, alternate leaves have 3–5 leaflets on long petioles; the end leaflet is typically larger. Leaflets are up to 5" long and 3" wide, ovate, with coarsely toothed margins; their undersurface is usually paler and slightly pubescent. Flowers form on racemes longer than they are wide, blooming April–June. Each raceme typically has 10–20 flowers, each with 5 oval white petals, 5 pointed sepals, and numerous stamens. Shiny, purplish-black aggregate fruits are around ¾" long, globe shaped to cylindrical, appearing in late June–August.

Dewberry (*R. flagellaris*) is similar to blackberry but has shorter, low-trailing vines, smaller leaves, larger flowers, and larger fruits that ripen earlier; it is often found in grassland habitats.

Common blackberry

Black raspberry (*R. occidentalis*) has round, green to purplish arching canes and smaller, straight thorns. The surface of the stems often has a whitish bloom that rubs off; this can be harvested by rubbing the stems in a bit of water and using the water in ferments as a natural yeast. Compound leaves tend to be trifoliate, with white undersides. The soft fruit is easily removed, leaving the torus on the stem and a thimble-like depression in the fruit.

Habitat/Range: Found in woodland borders, valleys, fencerows, abandoned pastures, glades, savannahs, old fields, thickets, and along roadsides. Range is throughout the eastern half of the United States, west to Oklahoma, Kansas, and Nebraska. It is introduced to California and British Columbia, absent from most Gulf Coast states. Numerous *Rubus* species are present throughout the United States except for the shortgrass prairie regions.

Uses: Eat on the spot, or collect for use in pies, cobblers, jams, syrups, wine, brandy, or topping for any dessert or confection. Can be dried and used in pemmican and trail mix. The leaves make a nice tea and can be used in higher doses as treatment for diarrhea. Flower petals can be added to salads or drinks. The leaves and fruit have great health benefits and are used medicinally to treat various ailments.

Warnings/Comments: There are over a dozen species of *Rubus* (mostly blackberry/raspberry types) found in the central grasslands, many of which can interbreed and hybridize. Several species have been developed into thornless, larger-fruited varieties and cultivated around the world.

Black raspberry

RUBIACEAE (BEDSTRAWS, MADDERS, COFFEES)

This cosmopolitan family contains around 13,500 species in about 620 genera, many occurring in the tropics or subtropics. It consists of terrestrial trees, shrubs, lianas, or herbs that are recognizable by simple, opposite, or whorled leaves. Economically important species include coffee (*Coffea*), the antimalarial alkaloid quinine (*Cinchona*), dye plants (*Rubia*), and ornamental cultivars such as *Gardenia*.

FRAGRANT BEDSTRAW
Galium triflorum and others

Edible parts/harvest time: Leaves, stems, and roots in spring through summer. Native.
Description: This herbaceous perennial is 1–3' tall with occasional branches that tend to sprawl. Stems are ridged with sparse short hairs, light green to reddish green in color, with whorls of 6 sessile leaves forming at intervals along the stem. Leaves are up to 2½" long and ½" wide, oblanceolate with short, pointed tips; margins are smooth or ciliate. Developing from the middle to upper whorled leaves are 1–3 axillary or terminal stalks of flowers, each producing 1–3 flowers on slender pedicels. Blooms May–August; individual flowers are about ⅛" across with 4 greenish-white to white petals that taper to narrow tips, 4 stamens, and a bristly 2-celled ovary. Flowers mature to bristly carpels less than ½" across that attach easily to passing objects.

Cleavers (*G. aparine*) is similar but has longer, slender leaves with pointed tips and 8 leaves per whorl. Hooked bristles on its leaves and weak stems cause it to easily break off and cling onto clothing. Licorice bedstraw (*G. circaezens*) is a shorter, more erect species with 4 whorled leaves that are broad and short.

Habitat/Range: Fragrant bedstraw occurs in damp areas of prairies, bases of rocky bluffs, thickets, moist meadows, partially shaded seeps and springs, and along streambanks and roadsides. Cleavers may occur in the same habitat but also in disturbed ground, croplands, pastures, and waste areas. Both species' range is throughout the United States, but they are

Licorice bedstraw with (inset) cleavers

less common or absent in dry western grasslands and shortgrass prairie. Licorice bedstraw is generally found in more shaded habitats in the central to eastern half of the United States.

Uses: Fragrant bedstraw has a distinctive sweet, vanilla-like scent when dried and can be used as a flavorful tea or for a vanilla flavoring. Young shoots and tender tops of these and several other *Galium* species can be finely chopped and used in salads or cooked whole as a potherb, but cooking may remove some of the health benefits. Licorice bedstraw does have a licorice-like flavor, but a few species may be bitter. Cleavers may be too bristly for use in salads, but its watery stems are great to put in a juicer, or chopped and soaked in water overnight for a healthy decoction. The seeds of bedstraws can be dried, roasted, and ground as a coffee substitute. The vanilla-like scent of several *Galium* species made them a favored plant to stuff mattresses—thus the name bedstraw. *Galium* species have been used throughout history for medicine. The juice was extracted to treat insect bites, burns, rashes, and other skin conditions.

Warnings/Comments: Fragrant bedstraw's sweet vanilla aroma comes from the antioxidant agent coumarin, which also provides many of its medicinal properties. Pharmacological studies show that extracts of *G. aparine* possess antimicrobial, anticancer, and hepatoprotective effects. *G. odoratum* (sweet woodruff) is a European species cultivated for medicinal herb gardens.

RECIPE

WILD MOCK VANILLA EXTRACT (FROM ALAN BERGO'S BOOK *THE FORAGER CHEF*)

Dry fairly large bundles of fragrant bedstraw stems with leaves in a low oven. Pack them in a jar, cover with quality vodka or good moonshine, and let sit for a few days. Squeeze the liquid out and discard the stems, replace them with a new batch of dried stems and leaves, and let sit for another few days. Strain, heat a bit in a double boiler, and bottle.

SOLANACEAE (NIGHTSHADES, TOMATOES, PEPPERS, POTATOES)

This economically important family consists of about 2,700 species in 98 genera, including many of our food plants such as potatoes, tomatoes, tomatillos, eggplants, and chili peppers. The family also includes jimsonweed (*Datura* spp.), mandrake (*Mandragora* spp.), deadly nightshade (*Atropa belladonna*), and tobacco (*Nicotiana* spp.), all containing toxic alkaloids with medicinal or psychotropic properties. Consumption of these toxins may be deadly in the short term, or in the long term, as with tobacco.

GROUND CHERRY (AKA WILD TOMATILLO, HUSK TOMATO)
Physalis longifolium and others

Edible parts/harvest time: Ripe fruits in late summer through late fall. Native.

Description: This curious-looking perennial produces sweet/tart berries covered in a papery husk. It may be difficult to locate hidden among other plants, but it is unmistakable when the lantern-like husked fruits are present. Stem is green to purplish and branched, up to 2½' tall, with alternate, ovate leaves up to 5" long (usually smaller) on long petioles. Leaf margins are entire or with lobe-like, irregular teeth. Blooms May–September, with yellow, bell-shaped flowers forming singly at the leaf and flower axils. Individual flowers are about 1" across, with 5 purplish spots appearing as a ring at the base of the corolla. Fruits are encased in a drooping green or purplish husk that is 5-sided with a pointed tip and 1–1½" long. The fleshy berry inside is about ¼" across, ripening to yellow, greenish yellow, or purple, depending on the species.

Black nightshade (*Solanum* spp.) has somewhat similar foliage, but its leaves are generally more dentate, smooth, and on winged petioles. It has small, white, 5-petaled flowers with yellow stamens that form on umbels, and round, edible black berries without husks. Several nightshade species are native to the central grasslands, including American (*Solanum interius*) and eastern (*S. ptychanthum*); both were formerly lumped with the old-world species *S. nigrum*. Older sources report the black fruits as toxic, possibly because of the plant's resemblance to the highly toxic deadly nightshade (*Atropa belladonna*). Black

Black nightshade VINAYARAJ, WIKIMEDIA COMMONS

nightshade has a long history of use wherever it occurs; the ripe fruits are safe and delicious when cooked in jellies and syrups. The leaves of some species are eaten as potherb greens but may have varying regional levels of toxicity; use with caution. **Spiny, yellow-fruited species such as horse nettle (*S. carolinense*) are toxic and should be avoided—be sure of identification.**

Habitat/Range: Found in sunny to partly shaded disturbed areas, roadside ditches, pastures, cultivated fields, old fields, forest edges, savannas, ledges, open bluffs, and occasionally in bottomland and upland forest. Range is throughout the lower 48 states, north into Ontario and Quebec.

Uses: Ripe fruits are delicious raw or cooked; some describe the flavor as slightly pineapple-tomato. Add to soups or cooked dishes, use in salsas and sweet or savory sauces, or cook fruits with pectin to make a great jam. To freeze fresh berries for later use, place them on a flat pan spaced to where they don't touch. Put the pan into the freezer; when the berries are frozen, transfer them to a freezer bag to store. During one foraging class, we crushed raw ground cherries for a zesty pizza sauce on an acorn-flour crust and topped it with hazelnuts, roasted wild onion, wild plums, and toasted grasshoppers.

Warnings/Comments: Use only when berries are sweet, soft, and fully ripe. Unripe berries may cause stomach irritation and could cause sickness if consumed in excess. The leaves and stems of all Solanaceae may be somewhat toxic, even though some species are regularly consumed. If the berries are bitter after cooking, do not consume. Around a dozen native species of *Physalis* occur in the central grasslands.

ROASTED GROUND CHERRY AND TOMATO SALSA

1½–2 cups ripe ground cherries, husked

2–3 small to medium Roma tomatoes, sliced in half lengthwise

1 jalapeño or your favorite hot pepper, sliced in half lengthwise

½ medium to large red onion, coarsely chopped

2 cloves garlic, finely chopped

Extra virgin olive oil

¼ cup cilantro

1 small lime, juiced

Salt to taste

1. Place tomatoes and pepper skin side up with the ground cherries, onion, and garlic in a shallow pan lined with aluminum foil; lightly drizzle with olive oil.

2. Place in a broiler oven or grill till the skins char, making sure everything gets a little blackened.

3. Chop the roasted ingredients into moderately fine pieces, or put in a food processor and pulse several times until coarsely mixed (not soupy).

4. Put roasted ingredients in a saucepan, add cilantro, lime juice, and salt to taste. Simmer 6–7 minutes.

5. Let cool before serving; best if left overnight in the refrigerator to allow flavors to blend.

URTICACEAE (NETTLES)
This family has worldwide distribution and comprises about 2,625 species grouped into 53 genera. Many have stinging hairs on the surfaces of stems and leaves.

WOOD NETTLE, STINGING NETTLE
Laportea canadensis, Urtica dioica

Wood nettle

Edible parts/harvest time: Shoots and tender top leaves in spring. Seeds in late summer and fall. Native.

These delicious, often unwelcome plants are often located first by touch. Take a bare-legged stroll through weedy vegetation near riparian bottomlands and you'll know when you find it. The hollow hairs on the leaves and stems act as tiny hypodermic needles that inject a mix of formic acid and other alkaloids into the skin, causing a short-lived itchy rash. Fortunately, a couple of antidote plants are usually nearby. Jewelweed (*Impatiens capensis*) and curly dock (*Rumex crispus*) leaves crushed with the juice rubbed on the rash will quickly relieve the itch.

Stinging nettle

Wood nettle seeds; (inset) shoot at collection stage

Description: Wood nettle has unbranched, hairy stalks that are 2–5' tall. Leaves are on long petioles, spaced alternately on the zigzagged upper third of the stalk. Individual leaves are 3–7" long, hairy, broadly ovate, with coarsely toothed margins. Seedheads form as small clusters at leaf axils, often forming a larger panicle at the stem apex. Small, leaflike append-ages hold tiny seeds on the underside. Stinging nettle (*Urtica dioica*) has pairs of opposite, slender leaves along the stem.

Habitat/Range: Nettles like rich, moist soil where rhizomes can spread to form large colo-nies in wooded stream and river bottoms, shaded deep hollows, bases of slopes, swamps, and near wooded ponds. Wood nettle ranges throughout eastern and central North Amer-ica; stinging nettle is found throughout the country but is less common in the Southeast.

Uses: Emerging in spring, shoots are great as a cooked vegetable; newer leaves and tender tops of mature plants can be used as a potherb or in soups till the seed clusters appear in late summer to fall. The stinging hairs are softened after a short boil. An infusion of dry leaves makes a nice tea. Seeds can be used as a grain, collected by drying the tops and shak-ing over a flat surface. To eat raw leaves, pick a tender top leaf, roll it into a tight tube, and tightly roll the length of the tube to crush the glands containing the toxin. I was skeptical at first, but it works! The tough, outer skin on the stalks can be stripped for use as a supe-rior cordage fiber. Stinging nettle can be prepared similarly to wood nettle but may have a stringy texture. Both species have numerous medicinal properties.

Warnings/Comments: To avoid the stinging hairs, collect with gloves or use large leaves to wrap and protect your hands.

RECIPE

WOOD OR STINGING NETTLE HUMMUS

1–2 cups fresh and tender nettle tops and leaves

1 (12-ounce) can chickpeas, drained and rinsed

2 tablespoons extra virgin olive oil

1 lemon, juiced (or substitute 2–3 tablespoons strong sumac berry tea for tartness)

1–2 tablespoons well-stirred tahini (or substitute wild nut butter)

1 tablespoon finely chopped wild or store-bought garlic

¼ teaspoon ground cumin (or substitute wild carrot or other wild seeds)

Sea salt to taste

1. Bring a pot of water to a boil, place nettles in for around a minute, then drain and set aside. Keep the liquid for tea or stock.

2. Add half each of the chickpeas, oil, and lemon juice (or sumac tea) to the food processor, process for 1 minute, then scrape down the sides.

3. Add remaining chickpeas and half each of the oil and tahini and process for 1–2 minutes or until thick and smooth; scrape down the sides again.

4. Add the spices, nettle leaves, and remaining tahini and lemon and process to desired consistency. If the hummus is too thick. slowly add 2–3 tablespoons of water while blending until the consistency is right.

5. Serve topped with edible wildflowers or chopped wild greens.

PELLITORY (AKA CUCUMBERWEED)
Parietaria pensylvanica

Edible parts/harvest time: Top leaves and stems in late spring through late summer. Native.

Similar toxic species: Three-seeded mercury, see "Warnings/Comments."

Description: This inconspicuous annual is about ½–1½' tall, with simple leaves and an unbranched central stem. Stem is 4-angled, green to reddish, and pubescent. Alternate leaves are up to 3½" long and ¾" across, lanceolate, finely pubescent, and with generally smooth margins. A major vein and 2 side veins are visible at the base of the upper leaf surface. Blooms midsummer, with small clusters of bracts and flowers forming at the axils of the middle to upper leaves. Each flower is surrounded by several green, hairy, linear bracts about ⅛" long that extend beyond the flowers. Staminate, pistillate, or perfect flowers can appear together in the same clusters. Flowers have green sepals and are without petals. A taste test will reveal its cucumber-like flavor.

Habitat/Range: Prefers partially to mostly shaded habitats in both natural and disturbed areas. Occurs in limestone glades, rocky slopes, thickets, savannas (under trees), along cliff bases, floodplains, and fencerows with woody vegetation, under yard trees, and in shaded areas along buildings and stone walls. Range is throughout much of the United States, less common in the Southeast and western coastal areas.

Uses: Pellitory's cucumber flavor makes it a great addition to salads, pesto, or any dish that needs a touch of green and extra flavor. The plant's slight hairiness isn't noticeable when it is collected young or chopped well and mixed with other ingredients. The plant can also be steamed or cooked, but this results in a milder flavor. European varieties have been used medicinally for thousands of years, noted for their diuretic properties.

Warnings/Comments: The somewhat toxic three-seeded mercury (*Acalypha virginica*) in the spurge family (Euphorbiaceae) may appear somewhat similar but has toothed leaves, a bushier appearance, and generally grows taller than pellitory. Its leaves and flower bracts turn a rich copper color later in the season, earning it the name copperleaf.

VIOLACEAE (VIOLETS)

The family's best-known genus, *Viola*, is herbaceous. Most of the other 806 species in 25 genera are shrubs or small trees. Many cultivar species are commercially available and sold as violets or pansies.

COMMON BLUE VIOLET
Viola sororia and others

Edible parts/harvest time: Flowers and young leaves whenever present. Native.

Description: A low-growing perennial that emerges from rhizomes as a basal rosette. Leaves are hairy, up to 3" long and 3" across, generally heart shaped, with blunt-serrate (scalloped) margins. They typically grow in bunches up to 4" tall and 6" across. Blooms March to June, and sporadically into fall. Flowers are borne singly on smooth stems and are usually taller than the leaves. Most species have 2 upright and 2 lateral bearded petals and a lower, nectar-holding small petal that serves as a landing spot for insects. Petal color can be dark blue to nearly white, with a pale lavender center and streaks at the throat.

Several species of *Viola* are found in the central grasslands, some exhibiting very different petal color and leaf forms than the heart-leaved *V. sororia*. All have similar flower structure and are edible.

Habitat/Range: Occurs in moist to mesic black-soil prairies, bottomland prairies, savannas, roadside ditches, rocky slopes, near ponds, lakes, and streams, and in open woodlands and their borders. In developed areas, it can be found in lawns, city parks, moist waste areas, and along hedges or near buildings. Numerous *Viola* species range throughout North America.

Uses: Raw flowers and young, tender leaves are a nutritious and beautiful salad addition. Leaves can be steamed, sautéed, and used in cooked dishes and as a thickener in soups. Flowers can be candied, jellied, added to pancakes and other cakes, used as a garnish, or frozen into ice cubes for drinks. Used medicinally to treat numerous ailments, both internal and external.

Warnings/Comments: Vitamin-rich violets may contain double the amount of vitamin C compared to citrus per weight and double the amount of vitamin A compared to spinach.

RECIPE

VIOLET/REDBUD FLOWER TART

2½ cups redbud or violet jelly (See eastern redbud for recipe)

3 cups coconut milk

3 pods star anise

3 teaspoons agar

½ teaspoon xanthan gum (optional)

1 teaspoon dried redbud or violet flowers, for garnish

Mix ingredients cold in a pan; heat slowly until mixture is hot in the middle and sets up on a frozen plate. Skim or strain out solids. Pour into molds and decorate with fresh violet, redbud, or other seasonal flower petals.

VITICEAE (GRAPES)
This family consists of 910 known species in 14 genera, most of which are tendril-bearing woody vines with fleshy fruits.

RIVER GRAPE
Vitis riparia and others

Edible parts/harvest time: Leaves in spring when tender. Fruits in fall. Native.

Toxic look-alikes: Canadian moonseed, see "Warnings/Comments."

Description: A perennial branching, woody vine, often climbing into high tree canopies. Older vines can become quite large, with dark reddish-brown shredding bark. Younger vines are gray or brown, with slight ridges. Nonwoody, climbing young stems are smooth, yellowish green to reddish, with tendrils opposite the leaves. Alternate leaves are generally palmate, orbicular to 3-lobed, with a pointed tip. Margins are broadly toothed, and the base is cleft at the petiole. Leaf blades can be up to 6" long and 5" across, but specimens found in grasslands are often smaller. Blooms May–June; clusters of tiny yellowish-green flowers form opposite new leaves on drooping panicles up to 5" long. In July–September, female flowers mature to drooping clusters of globoid bluish-purple fruits, each up to ⅜" across and containing several small, pear-shaped seeds.

At least 5 *Vitis* species occur in the central grasslands. The large, tough-skinned muscadine grape (*V. rotundifolia*) occurs in southeastern Oklahoma and east Texas; I didn't know it wasn't spelled "muskydime" until I read about it in a book.

Habitat/Range: Found in various conditions and habitats. Occurs in river bottom woodlands, cottonwood groves, bluff bases and ledges, borders of damp prairies and meadows, streambanks, fencerows, and brushy roadsides. Range is mostly the eastern and midwestern United States and Canada. Absent from Alabama to South Carolina and Florida in the east, and from the Desert Southwest to Idaho.

Uses: Great on the spot, made into jams, preserves, and syrups, or dried into raisins, but chiefly known for making wine. Always look for ground fall around high-reaching vines. Young, tender leaves can be added to salads or used as a flavoring for dill pickles; larger leaves can be steamed to make rolled Greek dolmas with fillings of your choice. Terrestrial runners and young vines make great basket material. The watery sap of larger vines can be used as an emergency pure water source in wetter months. Cut the vine as high as you can reach, then cut at the ground. Hold the cut section upright and collect the sap in containers. Seeds can be pressed to harvest grapeseed oil. The whitish boom on ripe fruits can be harvested as a sourdough yeast starter or used for other ferments.

Warnings/Comments: Raccoon grape/porcelain berry (*Amelopsis* spp.) is an inedible grape relative with similar fruits and leaves; its stems have a white pithy center and lenticels on the bark, and the somewhat toxic fruits ripen to different colors, from lilac to lavender or bluish. The toxic moonseed vine (*Minispermum canadense*) has palmately lobed leaves, but they lack the toothed leaf margins and forked tendrils of true grapes. Moonseed fruits contain a single, flattened seed with a small notch in the edge (like a cookie with a bite taken out). Hybridization between wild and cultivated grape varieties can make specific identification problematic, but wild species will contain the familiar pear-shaped seeds.

Monocots

ALISMATACEAE (ARROWHEADS, WATER PLANTAINS)

This cosmopolitan family comprises between 85 and 95 species in 11 genera. Most occur in temperate regions of the Northern Hemisphere and are found in aquatic habitats such as ponds and marshes. Several have edible rhizomes, leaves, and flower buds.

WAPATO (AKA COMMON ARROWHEAD, DUCK POTATO)
Sagittaria latifolia and others

Edible parts/harvest time: Corms in fall and winter. Leaves and flower stalks in spring and summer. Seedpods and rhizomes in fall. Native.

Similar toxic species: Arrow arum, see "Warnings/Comments."

Description: A semiaquatic, often colony-forming perennial with arrowhead-shaped basal leaves and 1 or more flowering stalks. Root system consists of fibrous rhizomes, occasionally producing numbers of starchy root corms. Leaves are on erect, stout petioles up to 20" tall, with blades up to 14" long and 10" across but often smaller and narrower. Blades have conspicuous, generally palmate parallel veins, smooth margins, and reverse-pointing basal lobes similar in length to or longer than the primary blade. The smooth, round flower stalk is often the same height to or slightly taller than the leaves, with several whorls of 2–3 flowers, 1–2" apart. Lower pistillate flowers form a bur-like bud that becomes a roundish seedhead. Upper staminate flowers are showy, with 3 rounded white petals surrounding a small globe of yellow stamens.

Habitat/Range: Found in shallow water or mud in mucky ditches, sloughs, seeps, marshes, borders of ponds, and along banks of slow-moving streams. Range is throughout the continental United States and Canada but may be absent from a few western states.

Uses: Corms are edible after peeling; best when boiled, baked, or roasted and used like potatoes. They can be candied, pickled, or sliced thin and dried or roasted for grinding into flour. Young, freshly unfurled leaves, petioles, and early flower stalks can be boiled as vegetables or used in cooked dishes. Flower petals make a nice nibble or salad garnish. The

Wapato corms SAMUEL THAYER

fall seedpods and fresh growth on tips of rhizomes can be eaten raw or cooked. They were traditionally harvested by wading barefoot into a partially submerged patch, locating the corms by feel with the feet, then using toes to dislodge them so they float to the surface. A garden rake is also useful, as the corms are often at different depths throughout the muck.

Warnings/Comments: Be 100 percent sure of identification! The similar arrow arum (*Peltandra virginica*) is an uncommon emergent aquatic with a leaf shape resembling arrowhead but with a prominent midrib and radiating pinnate veins, and flower structure (spathe and spadix) typical of arums. Its root was used for food by natives, but only after a long drying or cooking time. Arums typically have cell structures that contain calcium oxalate crystals (raphides) that may embed in your mouth and tongue when eaten raw. Its range is extreme southern Oklahoma and east Texas. There are 7 similar species of *Sagittaria* in the Midwest; a couple of related species have linear cattail-like leaves.

AMARYLLIDACEAE
(GARLICS, DAFFODILLS, AMARYLLIS)

This family has 70 to 75 genera with roughly 1,600 species of herbaceous, mostly perennial, bulbous, or rhizomatous flowering plants in the order Asparagales. Characteristics are linear leaves and symmetrical, umbellate flowers with tepals that may be fused at the base into a floral tube or a corona. Plants in the onion subfamily Allioideae produce allyl sulfide compounds that provide the characteristic onion odor.

CANADA ONION
Allium canadense and others

Edible parts/harvest time: Leaves in spring and early summer. Bulbs and bulblets whenever present. Native and introduced.

Description: An herbaceous perennial with long, slender, flat leaves emerging from a papery-sheathed bulb. Leaves are keeled, up to 12" long, usually emerging as a small rosette. A round, smooth flowering stem up to 3' emerges from older bulbs. The flower stem terminates in a teardrop-shaped bud covered in a papery membrane, eventually splitting to expose a dome-like flower head of white to pinkish star-shaped flowers and/or green to reddish aerial bulblets.

Fall glade onion (*A. stellatum*) and Drummond's onion (*A. drummondii*) are also found in prairie or glade habitats; both have showy purple flowers. The introduced field garlic (*A. vineale*) has long, hollow leaves and is found in the easternmost part of this book's range. All members of the genus *Allium* emit a strong onion or garlic odor when crushed except for false garlic (*Nothoscordum bivalve*). It was previously and erroneously considered toxic and placed within the Lily family, but later classification placed it with Alliums, and no present toxins have been identified.

Habitat/Range: Found in prairies, glades, roadsides, rocky slopes, woodland borders, croplands, waste areas, and disturbed habitats. Native to Europe, it has naturalized throughout

the eastern and midwestern United States and Canada, west to Oklahoma and Nebraska. Also found in the West Coast states and Montana.

Uses: Tender leaves can be chopped and used as chives. Bulbs and bulblets can be used as flavoring in raw or cooked dishes, dried and crushed for onion powder, or preserved in brine and pickled, much like any other garlic or onion.

Warnings/Comments: A smell test is valuable to aid in identification. Be aware of the look-alike and highly toxic Nuttal's death camas (*Toxicoscordion nuttallii*; see Poisonous Plants chapter) that has no garlic smell. Death camas will typically have a larger bulb with dark brown skin. (If you have no sense of smell, best to avoid or get confirmation of species with someone who can detect onion odor.) Wild onion can be an agricultural pest, and it can taint cow's milk when included in their forage.

False wild garlic

Field garlic tops

Field garlic bulbs

RECIPE

WILD ONION SEASONING ASH

This simple process is an ancient way to preserve the flavor of strong herbs like garlic or onion and can be used in various ways. Other savory wild or cultivated herbs can be added to make a seasoning mix.

1. Place bundles of wild onion tops or other flavorful seasoning greens in a shallow pan and bake at 425°F for about 3 minutes. Turn and bake another 3 minutes, until all are a rich brownish black but not yet smoking. Thicker plants like store-bought onions and thick-leaved herbs will need to be baked longer.

2. After cooling, pulverize with a molcajete, mortar and pestle, or coffee grinder.

3. Store in airtight containers.

Use the ash to dust meats and vegetables before roasting, or add to soups and cooked dishes. Make paints or drizzles by mixing 1–2 teaspoons of ground plant ash with 2 teaspoons walnut oil and ½ teaspoon sea salt. Brush on or drizzle over baked breads, meats, vegetables, or other savory cooked dishes.

ASPARAGACEAE (YUCCAS, HYACINTHS, ASPARAGUS)

Asparagaceae includes 114 genera with a total of approximately 2,900 known species; the family name is based on garden asparagus, *Asparagus officinalis*. This family includes familiar houseplants such as hosta, snake plant, and spider plant; garden plants such as garlics and asparagus; and desert plants in the subfamily Agavoideae such as agaves and yuccas.

EASTERN CAMAS (AKA WILD HYACINTH)
Camassia scilloides and others

Edible parts/harvest time: Bulbs in late summer to fall. Native.

Toxic look-alikes: Nuttal's death camas, see "Warnings/Comments."

Description: This attractive perennial produces a roundish root bulb up to 1½" across, often forming large colonies. Grass-like, linear leaves emerge as a basal rosette and are smooth with smooth margins, up to 12" long and less than ½" wide, with a prominent mid-rib and pointed at the tip. Blooms April–May with an erect, smooth central flower stalk up to 2' tall, terminating in a raceme-like cluster of up to 50 flowers; 2–3 bract-like leaves often form below the flowers. Individual flowers are ¾–1" across, each with a bright green central ovary, yellow anthers, and 6 narrow petals that are pale blue or lavender, rarely white.

Prairie camas (*C. angusta*) is similar and may be difficult to differentiate; it blooms about a month later and has generally shorter flower petals.

Habitat/Range: Found in moist prairies, glades, old fields, rich upland and bottomland forests, moist savannas and open woodlands, bluff ledges, and along streambanks. Occurs throughout the eastern United States, west to Texas and Kansas, north to Ontario, east to Pennsylvania and Georgia. Absent from Florida.

Uses: The starchy bulbs can be eaten raw but consuming too many will turn you into a fart machine. Their high content of indigestible inulins must be broken down by cooking or drying into digestible sugars, which also gives them a great nutty-sweet flavor. The bulbs were traditionally harvested by indigenous tribes just after the flowering stage and baked in large pits for up to 2 days. To cook them them at home, wrap them in large edible or savory leaves like grape or cup rosinweed with a dash of water and cooked in a slow cooker on low for 24–48 hours. They can also be slow-roasted, boiled, dried, or used in soups or other cooked dishes, as well as crushed into paste, dried, and ground to a powder for storage. When bulbs are properly prepared, the flavor is potato-like but nutty and almost as sweet as figs. They can be harvested any time in the growing season but are sweetest when harvested after the tops have wilted.

Warnings/Comments: Take care with identification to separate wild hyacinth from the similar but highly toxic Nuttal's death camas (*Toxicoscordion nuttallii*), which is occasionally

Eastern camas bulb

present in the same habitat. The two are easily distinguished when in bloom, but bulbs encountered without foliage are more difficult to differentiate. *T. nuttalli* has white flower petals that are shorter and broader, and on longer pedicels (up to 1" long) than *Camassia* (see Poisonous Plants chapter). Identify when blooming or look for the longer pedicels on dried tops to make sure all plants in the entire colony are *Camassia*. Do not consume unless identification is 100 percent positive! As with all native roots, tubers, and bulbs, collect only when encountered in large colonies, harvest no more than 10–15 percent of the colony, and pick off and replant smaller bulblets if present. This beautiful native does well in edible flower gardens.

RECIPE

CAMAS AND SWEET ONION SALSA

This basic salsa recipe features the nutty flavor of camas and is the perfect side or topping for salmon or other wild game.

¾ cup chopped roasted camas bulbs (or rehydrated dried camas)

½ cup chopped sweet onion

1 teaspoon whole yellow mustard seeds

½–1 teaspoon rice vinegar or cider vinegar

Table or sea salt and ground black pepper to taste

Optional: Chopped chili pepper to taste

Mix all ingredients and serve, or refrigerate for up to a week.

SOLOMON'S SEAL
Polygonatum biflorum and look-alikes

Solomon's seal

Edible parts/harvest time: Tender shoots in April and May. Berries are toxic. Native.

Description: An elegant, herbaceous perennial with a single, slightly zigzagged stem emerging from rhizomes. Stem is unbranched, round and smooth, usually arching up 3' or longer. Pale green, alternate leaves are up to 5" long and 2½" wide, sessile, ovate to elliptic, smooth, with prominent parallel veins and smooth margins. Flowers appear in May–June, typically occurring in pairs that droop from the stem on short peduncles at leaf axils. Individual flowers are pale green to white, consisting of a narrow, tubular corolla up to ¾" long, with 6 short lobes surrounding the rim. Fertilized flowers produce a round, bluish-purple inedible berry that is about ½" across.

False Solomon's seal (*Maianthemum racemosum*) is sometimes mistaken for Solomon's seal when first emerging; it has similar uses and a similar stem/leaf structure but with a showy white flower cluster at the stem terminus. Flowers mature to spherical, red to purplish edible berries with a nice sweet/tart flavor.

Habitat/Range: Occurs in moist prairies, moist rocky slopes, thickets, rich bottomlands or woodlands, streambanks, roadsides, wooded valleys and ravines, and shaded seeps and springs. Range is the eastern half of Oklahoma, Kansas, and Nebraska, and scattered locations in the Dakotas. Commonly found in proper habitats in the eastern half of the United States and Canada.

Uses: Young, tender shoots can be eaten raw in salads, cooked as a vegetable, or used in soups and other cooked dishes. Best collected when the leaves are still curled around the stem. Flavor varies geographically; discard leaves if they are bitter. Older stems can become fibrous. Smaller rhizomes are edible in soups and other cooked dishes and can be dried and ground for a flour additive. Most are too tough and fibrous to mess with, so best to leave them for future growth.

Warnings/Comments: Solomon's seal berries are reportedly toxic and should not be consumed. As with all natives, avoid harvesting unless found in quantity, and always leave plenty for future growth.

False solomon's seal with berries

PLAINS YUCCA (AKA SMALL SOAPWEED)
Yucca glauca and others

Edible parts/harvest time: Young shoots and flowers in May and June. Fruits in July and August. Native.

Yuccas may top the list of useful plants, providing medicine, cordage fiber, hearth and spindle for friction fire, soap, sewing needles, and three types of food.

Description: This colony-forming perennial appears as a clump of lance-like stiff leaves with sharp tips, each up to 3' long and ½" wide, emerging in a rosette from a thickened underground stem. The leaves appear longitudinally curved with a concave upper surface, and are smooth except for long whitish hairs along the margins. A stout flower stalk emerges from the rosette's center, at first appearing like a large asparagus sprout. Blooms late May–July, with nodding bell-shaped flowers appearing on short branches along the top two-thirds of the stalk. Each flower has 3 petals and 3 similar sepals that are pale greenish to cream white, about 1½" long and 3" across. Flowers mature to 6-sided dry fruits up to 3" long and 1–2" across, each enclosing 3 capsules containing many flat, black seeds.

Y. flaccida (Adam's needle or weak-leaved yucca) and *Y. filamentosa* (Spanish bayonet) are larger species with wider, floppier leaves; both are present in the eastern parts of the central grasslands as escaped or naturalized ornamentals.

Yucca shoot

Habitat/Range: Occurs in dry, rocky, or sandy well-drained prairies, pastures, slopes, and roadsides. Range is throughout the central Great Plains and the western edge of the Midwest prairies, from Texas and New Mexico to eastern Montana and the western half of the Dakotas.

Uses: Raw flowers are a good addition to salads; older flowers can be steamed, boiled, or added to cooked dishes. Young flower stalks can be boiled or roasted over embers and eaten like asparagus. Older stalks at pre-flowering stage can be cut into sections, roasted, and peeled. Young fruits can be boiled, roasted, or fried. Specimens in the eastern parts of its range may have higher saponin levels than those in the west, increasing the plant's bitterness. Due to these saponins, soap can be made by pounding the root. Leaf fibers make excellent cordage, and the dried flower stalk is one of the best materials for hand-drill or bow-drill friction fire materials. Whole yucca leaves can be plaited into hats, visors, and sandals. A sewing needle can be made by stripping the outer leaf fibers away from the center, leaving 6–8 individual fibers attached to the sharp tip. The fibers are gathered into two bundles and corded from the tip into a stout string.

Warnings/Comments: The sap can cause skin irritation due to the saponin content. Don't cut it with a chain saw to avoid getting the sap on your skin or in your eyes. The large roots of some *Agave* species are used to make tequila, pulque, and mezcal. Some are valued for their fibers; others are pit-roasted for consumption. Their drought hardiness and showy flowers make them quite popular for xeriscaping.

PANKO-CRUSTED YUCCA FRUITS

2–4 cups sliced yucca fruits

1–2 tablespoon olive oil

1–2 cloves minced garlic

1 tablespoon butter, melted

1 cup panko (more or less)

Seasoned salt and pepper to taste

1. Blanch the sliced fruits for 3–5 minutes, then move to a cutting board after cooled and pat them dry.

2. Heat a skillet, add a bit of olive oil and the garlic; cook till garlic is translucent and set aside.

3. Place dry sliced fruits in a bowl, drizzle them with melted butter, then put them in a bag with the panko and shake till they have a good coating.

4. Fry in the skillet with the cooked garlic, turning once to brown both sides. Remove to a plate covered with a paper towel, use another paper towel to mop up excess oil.

ASPHODELACEAE (DAYLILLIES, ALOES)

This family was recently split from the Lilies (Liliaceae) and includes around forty genera with about 900 known species occurring throughout the tropics and temperate zones. It includes many cultivated species used for ornamentals and cut flowers. Aloe vera is one species cultivated for its medicinal leaf sap.

ORANGE DAY LILY (AKA DITCH LILY)
Hemerocallis fulva

Edible parts/harvest time: Leaf shoots in spring. Buds and flowers in late spring to mid-summer. Roots in winter. Introduced.

A big surprise in my early foraging was discovering that the ubiquitous ditch lily that grew in our yard was a very tasty edible. The sautéed or lacto-fermented buds are delectable.

Description: This introduced perennial forms fibrous roots with fleshy tubers, and its leaves emerge as a basal rosette. Basal leaves are up to 2' long, linear, with a partially folded midrib, parallel venation, and sword-like pointed tips. Leaves become arched at maturity. One or more stout, erect flower stems emerge from the center of the rosette. The stems are up to 5' tall, round, smooth, and unbranched till near the apex. Podlike, 3-segmented buds up to 5" long emerge at the terminal ends of the branched stem, forming blooms in May–August. Funnel-shaped flowers are dull orange, up to 5½" across, with 6 deflexed petals. Each flower lasts only a day.

Habitat/Range: Found in old flower gardens, abandoned homesites, cemeteries, fields, thickets, roadsides, and disturbed streambanks; widely planted as an ornamental. Occurs throughout North America and eastern Canada, absent from California, Nevada, and the Desert Southwest. Native to Eurasia, with global anthropogenic distribution due to cultivation.

Uses: The white portion at the base of the innermost young leaves has a sweet flavor when eaten raw. Young leaves and shoots can be added to salads. Young-growth flower stems can be cut into segments and cooked as a vegetable. Unopened flower buds have a slight radish-like bite and are delicious raw, even better as a side dish after a quick sauté in butter. Mature flowers can be added to soups as a thickener or fried in tempura batter for fritters. Young, soft tubers are excellent when sautéed, boiled, or roasted.

Warnings/Comments: Some report a laxative effect if eaten in large quantity. Reported to cause allergic reactions in some, so consume sparingly the first time. Some true lilies in the genus *Lilium* are toxic. They grow from a root bulb instead of tubers, with leaves occurring up the flower stalk and flowers that last more than a day. To confuse the matter, *Hemerocallis* species are sometimes erroneously referred to as tiger lily, a *Lilium* species. More than 60,000 cultivars have been bred from the genus, not all of which are edible.

COMMELINACEAE (DAYFLOWERS, SPIDERWORTS)

This herbaceous family comprises 41 genera and 731 known species found in both the Old and New Worlds, several of which are grown ornamentally. Their flowers are short-lived, most lasting less than a day.

WHITEMOUTH DAYFLOWER
Commelina erecta and others

Edible parts/harvest time: Leaves, stems, and flowers whenever present and still tender. Native and introduced.

Description: An herbaceous, sprawling or erect native annual with stems up to 2' long. Stems are round and smooth, with slightly swollen nodes that can take root. Alternate leaves are ovate to lanceolate, sessile, or clasping at the stem, up to 5" long and 2" wide, with smooth margins and pointed tips. Flowers appear in May–October, borne singly on 1–2" stalks forming at the leaf axil. Each flower is ½–1" across, with 2 erect bright blue petals and a small, pale lower petal. Protruding from the center of the flower are 3 yellow upper staminodes, 2–3 short lower stamens, and a white style. The flower emerges from a curved, folded spathe, developing into a seedpod containing 2 or more seeds.

Habitat/Range: Found in bottomlands, moist forest borders, roadsides, croplands, lawns, gardens, moist fencerows, near dwellings, and along roadsides. Prefers damp, disturbed habitats, but can colonize wherever conditions permit. Range is the eastern United States and Canada, west to southern Arizona, western Nebraska and South Dakota. The similar Asiatic dayflower (*C. communis*) is native to Asia and found nearly globally due to anthropogenic distribution.

Uses: Young, tender stems and leaves are sweet and slightly mucilaginous; can be chopped and eaten raw in salads, steamed or boiled as a potherb, or added to stir-fries, soups, and other cooked dishes. Used medicinally for thousands of years in China due to its unique compounds and qualities. The plant is grown commercially in Japan to make commelinin, a complex blue pigment derived from the flower petals that was historically preferred by artists.

Warnings/Comments: There are several species of dayflower, and all are somewhat similar. Different varieties can intergrade, making species identification difficult. Occasionally cultivated as an ornamental, some species of dayflower can spread quickly to become a garden or agricultural pest.

OHIO SPIDERWORT (AKA BLUEJACKET)
Tradescantia ohiensis and others

Edible parts/harvest time: Shoots, leaves, and flowers in spring to midsummer. Seeds in late summer. Native.

Description: A clump-forming, herbaceous perennial with a smooth, zigzag stem up to 3' tall. Alternate, arching blue-green leaves are up to 15" long and 1" across. They are widest at the base and thinner at the tip, with a fold at the midrib, clasping the stem at thick nodes. Blooms May–July, with short-lived flowers appearing a few at a time in umbel-like clusters at the stem apex. Individual flowers are triangle shaped, up to 1½" across. Each flower has 3 rounded petals and 6 bright yellow anthers at the center that are surrounded by a small cluster of fine, deep blue filaments. Colors can vary to blue, lavender, purple, rose, and occasionally white.

Two other spiderwort species can be found in grassland habitats: the similar western spiderwort (*T. occidentalis*) and the low-growing, long-bracted spiderwort (*T. bracteata*).

Habitat/Range: Found in open to shady conditions in prairies, glades, old fields, pastures, bluff openings, savannas, openings and borders in upland forest, and disturbed ground along roadsides and railways. Range is the eastern United States and Ontario, west to Texas and Nebraska.

Uses: Shoots, young stems, and whole flower clusters can be eaten raw in salads, pickled, cooked as vegetables, or used in soups and other cooked dishes. Leaves can be used similarly but have a mucilaginous quality and can get astringent and less palatable with age. Flowers can be candied or used to make jelly.

Long-bracted spiderwort

Seeds can be roasted and ground for a flour additive, but some may be slightly bitter. Used medicinally for many ailments. The mucilaginous sap is used to treat insect bites and skin conditions. The root is used as a laxative.

Warnings/Comments: The midwestern prairie region is home to around 8 *Tradescantia* species. The Japanese geneticist Dr. Sadao Ichikawa discovered that the flowers of some species could detect minute amounts of gamma rays more accurately than a mechanical dosimeter. The blue filaments surrounding the stamens turned pink when subjected to amounts of radiation as small as 150 millirems. All *Tradescantia* species can contain needle-like calcium oxalate crystals (raphides) in their internal tissues but are rarely reported to cause skin irritation.

CYPERACEAE (SEDGES)

This large, grasslike family has 5,500 known species described in about ninety genera, with water chestnut and papyrus sedge being two of its better-known species. Stems are characteristically triangular in cross section; leaves are spirally arranged in three ranks.

YELLOW NUTSEDGE (AKA CHUFA NUT, TIGER NUTSEDGE)
Cyperus esculentus and others

Edible parts/harvest time: Tubers and seeds in early to late summer. Native, potentially aggressive.

Description: A colony-forming, grass-like sedge with long, slender leaves and an erect, central stem up to 2' tall. The rhizomes often form small, round, or elongated tubers. Leaf blades are produced in 3s and are connected by sheaths around the lower segment of stem. Each leaf is up to 1½" long and ½" wide, gradually tapering to a sharp point, with a distinct channel on the upper surface midrib. Flowers appear in midsummer or fall as a cluster of yellow floral spikelets in an umbel or compound umbel at the main stem terminus and on the ends of variable-length branches. Flowers mature to tri-cornered, flattened ovoid seeds.

Purple nutsedge (*C. rotundus*) is originally from India but has purplish flowers and less flavorful tubers. Some compare its flavor to menthol VapoRub, but it can be improved by soaking in water for a few days then drying.

Habitat/Range: Found in moist or disturbed areas, in gardens, lawns, fields, prairies, ditches, wetlands, and borders of ponds, lakes, and streams. Range is throughout the Eastern Hemisphere, most of the continental United States, and Canada. Absent from Wyoming and Montana.

Uses: The nutlike tubers have a sweet, slightly hazelnut-almond flavor and can be eaten raw, candied, boiled, or roasted, used to make a sweet *horchata*-like beverage, or as an almond

Young nutsedge tubers

substitute or a chocolate/coffee extender in confections. Tubers can be dried, ground, and used for flour. Seeds are edible and can be cooked as a cereal or dried and ground into flour. The tuber is popular in West Africa to make porridges and beverages. The strained material after making beverages can be used with or without other flours to make doughs for various uses. Nutsedge's amino acid profile is complementary to grains and legumes; together they make a complete protein. Soaking in water for at least 6 hours reduces the level of tannins and phenols. A larger cultivar is sold commercially as "tiger nuts."

Warnings/Comments: Due to its aggressively colonizing nature, nutsedge is listed as an agricultural or horticultural pest in some areas. Researchers found that a single nutsedge plant could grow enough seeds for 1,900 plants and produce 7,000 tubers in a year, making it one of the highest yield-per-acre starch crops. It was widely cultivated as a food crop in ancient Egypt and in most of Europe, and it is being rediscovered today as an alternative, healthy food source that will grow in areas not productive for other crops. The tubers contain a type of starch that is a beneficial prebiotic fiber, helping burn fat and reduce hunger. Recent studies have found that its dietary-resistant starch may improve insulin sensitivity and help reduce elevated blood sugar levels. Related bulrushes in the genus *Scirpus* are also edible. Young spring shoots are good raw or cooked. Parched seeds can be eaten or mixed with pollen and ground into flour. Large rhizomes can be eaten raw or cooked.

NUTSEDGE *HORCHATA* (ADAPTED FROM IAN GIESBRECHT'S RECIPE AT OZARK MOUNTAIN JEWEL)

1 cup nutsedge tubers

7–8 cups water

¾–1 teaspoon ground cinnamon

2–3 tablespoons honey, agave nectar, or sweetener of choice

Dash of vanilla flavoring

1. Wash and scrub the tubers thoroughly; soak them overnight.

2. Add water to a saucepan with the tubers and other ingredients; bring to a low simmer for 5 minutes while stirring.

3. Transfer to a blender and blend until smooth.

4. Pour the milk mixture into a nut milk bag or several layers of cheesecloth and squeeze all the milk out.

5. Transfer milk to a large glass container and refrigerate until ready to drink. Serve chilled.

6. Save and dry the leftover pulp after straining to add to flours or to make porridge.

POACEAE (GRASSES)

Poaceae may be the most economically important plant family, consisting of around 780 genera and nearly 12,000 species. It includes native grasslands, domesticated cereal grains, bamboo, and species cultivated for lawns and pasture. It has diverse uses such as human/livestock food, building material, and ethanol biofuel. All have edible seeds, but many nondomesticated species may be difficult to process.

Grass stems are typically hollow except at the nodes and have narrow, alternate leaves borne in two ranks. The lower part of each leaf clasps the stem and forms a sheath, an adaptation allowing it to withstand frequent grazing.

REED CANARY GRASS
Phalaris arundinaceae and others

Edible parts/harvest time: Seeds, shoots, and roots in late summer and fall. Native, with introduced strains that may be invasive in wetlands.

Description: A cool-season perennial grass 2–7' tall with an erect, smooth stem and gradually tapering leaf blades, often growing in large clumps 2–3' across. It is early sprouting, aggressive, and strongly rhizomatous, often forming dense mats that tend to dominate wet, fertile areas. Alternate rough-textured leaves occur mostly along the lower half of the culm. The flat, hairless leaf blades are up to 10" long and ¾" across, green to grayish blue, with a prominent midrib and rough margins. The hairless leaf sheath is the same color as the blade, with an elongated ligule that is white and membranous. The culm terminates in a slender, compact panicle of spikelets up to 10" long and 2–3" across with lateral, erect branches. Green to purple flowers occur May–mid-June, eventually turning to beige; seeds are shiny brown in color.

Carolina maygrass (*P. caroliniana*) is a more southern species with edible seeds and similar leaves, but its node sheaths are hairy at the top. Stems terminate in dense, oval seedheads up to 3" long and ¾" wide, with spikelets that appear green and white striped when young. Carolina maygrass was one of the "forgotten foods" independently cultivated in North America prior to the arrival of other more popular foods such a maize, beans, and squash from Mexico and Mesoamerica. It was one of several species that were abandoned when newer foods arrived.

Habitat/Range: Reed canary grass occurs in damp prairies and meadows, marshes, fens, streambanks, ditches, pond edges, and prairie swales. It can occur in wet to dry habitats but grows best in fertile, moist to wet soils. It is native to temperate regions of Europe, Asia, and North America.

Uses: Young, tender roots can be eaten raw or cooked like potatoes, or can be dried, ground coarsely, and used as a cooked cereal. Young shoots can be eaten raw or cooked and used like bamboo shoots if collected before the leaves form. The partly unfolded leaves can be used as a potherb. In Japan, the dried young leaves are ground into a powder and mixed with other cereal flours to make dumplings. Seeds can be ground into a powder and used as a flour. The seed is rather small and difficult to remove from the husk, but it is quite nutritious. A sugar can be extracted from the stalks or wounded stems; it can be eaten raw or cooked and has a sweet, almost licorice-like flavor. The stems can be boiled in water and then the water boiled off to obtain the sugar. A sugary gum that exudes from the stems can be rolled into sweet balls. A powder extracted from the dried stems can be moistened and roasted like marshmallow. Stems may contain up to 5 percent sugar. Many native and introduced grass species have grains large enough to process, but each will have a specific method to remove the hulls. Some may not be worth the time and effort (see Appendix B: Getting Started).

Warnings/Comments: Reed canary grass has a circumpolar range, but genetic differences and cultivation factors make some strains more aggressive. Decades ago, a Eurasian ecotype was selected for its vigor and planted throughout the United States for forage and erosion control. It is now a problematic wetland invasive.

EASTERN GAMAGRASS
Tripsacum dactyloides

Edible parts/harvest time: Seeds from late June to early September. Native.

Description: This distant relative of maize is a warm-season perennial bunchgrass that often forms fountain-like clumps up to 9' tall and 4' wide. Alternate leaves are up to 2½" long and 1" wide, with a defined midrib. Flower heads appear in May, with 1–4 narrowly cylindrical flower spikes up to 10" long emerging terminally on each stem (culm). The male, pollen-bearing florets occur in pairs at the top part of each spike; the seed-bearing, female florets form at the bottom half or third. The female florets appear to be sunken into the stalk, and each floret produces a pair of purplish-pink to white stigma. The top male part of the spike often falls off intact, while seeds forming in the female portion fall off individually.

Habitat/Range: Occurs in upland or moist prairies, glades, savannas, old fields, cropland borders, bottomlands, streambanks, and in disturbed, open areas. Range is central Texas, Oklahoma, Kansas, southeast Nebraska, southern Iowa, and throughout the southern two-thirds of the eastern United States.

Uses: The grains are tough but have a slightly nutty flavor and can be popped like popcorn, cooked into cereal, or ground into mush or flour.

Warnings/Comments: Eastern gamagrass is referred to as "the ice cream of forage crops" since bison and cattle often tend to overgraze it to the exclusion of other surrounding forage material. It has a nearly 30 percent protein content and high levels of the essential amino acid methionine. It probably would have been domesticated into a cereal grain if not for its poor seed yields when compared to corn. It is another native grassland species that has declined after the plowing of the prairies, but efforts are under way to bring back this highly nutritious grain as a dual-purpose forage. Agronomists have developed at least 2 cultivars and are currently working on crossbreed hybrids to increase the yield.

SMILACACEAE (GREENBRIERS)
The family consists of a single genus with 255 known species occurring throughout many tropical and warm temperate regions. Most have woody roots and a climbing or vining form. Some have woody vining stems with thorns; others are herbaceous and thornless.

GREENBRIER (AKA CATBRIER, BLASPHEME VINE)
Smilax spp.

Edible parts/harvest time: Shoots and young leaves in late spring through summer. Berries of some species in fall. Roots in winter. Native.

While conducting songbird research fieldwork years ago, I fell while attempting to walk across the top of a 3-foot-high thicket of thorny greenbrier, taking a while to extricate myself. I was walking a road out when someone in a car slowed down, saw my bloodied neck and shirt, and sped off! A friend later asked if I'd been wrestling bobcats. Falling into a greenbrier thicket may prompt bad language, hence the name "blaspheme vine."

Description: The central grasslands are home to several *Smilax* species; all are stout, woody, green vines, most with thorns or spines. They often form thickets or climb trees and structures up to 25' using the tendrils at the base of leaf stalks. All species have alternate, simple leaves up to 5" long and 3" wide. Leaf blades are typically shiny green, heart shaped or lanceolate to oval, with smooth margins.

Carrionflower (*S. lasioneura*) lacks thorns, and the flowers have a scent reminiscent of rotting flesh. Common greenbrier (*S. rotundifolia*) is found mostly in Oklahoma and parts of Texas. Most species have small yellow-green flowers that form in umbel-like clusters arising from leaf axils; flowers mature to clusters of ¼" purplish-black berries.

Habitat/Range: Found in a variety of forested and open conditions. Occurs in thickets, fencerows, dry to mesic woodlands, glades, bluffs, old fields, and dry edges of bottoms. Range of the various species is from central Texas, Oklahoma, Kansas, Nebraska, and parts of the Dakotas, west to the foothills of the Rocky Mountains, and east throughout the eastern half of the United States.

Uses: Tender tips of shoots, tendrils, and young leaves are great as a trail snack or in salads. They can also be lightly steamed but don't tolerate much cooking or boiling. Add them as a topping to cooked dishes and soups after cooking; some describe the taste as reminiscent of asparagus. Harvest like asparagus: Start bending the stem a foot or so from the tip and collect what breaks off easily. Young, tender roots of most species are edible raw but are best when boiled or roasted. Larger roots can be dried or roasted and ground for use as a flour—if you can get them out of the ground without a backhoe. The root pulp was mixed with molasses, corn, and sassafras and/or sarsaparilla root (*Aralia* spp.), then allowed to ferment into the drink sarsaparilla. Smilax berry juice isn't particularly tasty raw, but it can be used for syrups and jellies.

Warnings/Comments: Roots and berries are used medicinally to treat various ailments and contain numerous healthful phytochemicals and compounds.

TYPHACEAE (CATTAILS)

This marsh-dwelling family consists of 51 species in 2 genera and is characterized by having two-ranked leaves and a brownish, compact spike of unisexual flowers.

COMMON CATTAIL
Typha latifolia and others

Mature cattail with leaf stem shoot

Edible parts/harvest time: Emerging leaf bases in spring. Stem shoots and hearts in late spring and early summer. Stems, green heads, and pollen heads in mid- to late summer. Roots any time, best in fall. Native.

It would take a small book to thoroughly describe all the uses of cattail; it is truly nature's supermarket!

Description: A tall, colony-forming wetland perennial with long, narrow leaves and a brown, sausage-like flower spike; 6 or more erect or arching leaves up to 7' long and 1" across emerge from an oval core. A slender, round flower stalk up to 8' tall emerges from the center of the core, developing a terminal, cylindrical flower spike divided into 2 parts. The narrow, upper staminate spike develops pollen and withers away soon after flowering. The lower pistillate spike is up to 1½' long and 1½" across, maturing to the familiar brown seedhead we know as a cattail. In late fall, the flower heads explode into seedbearing white fluff for wind distribution.

Habitat/Range: Associated with open conditions, water-saturated soil/mud, or standing/ slow-moving water up to 1½' deep. Forms extensive colonies in marshes, sloughs, edges of ponds and lakes, and wet ditches. Occurs throughout the United States and Canada.

Uses: The white base of inner, emerging leaves is sweet and slightly cucumber flavored, and is great as a trail nibble. Larger leaf clusters can be peeled of outer leaves to expose the white core (called Cossack asparagus), which is eaten raw or cooked. The young, green flower head and lower stalks can be cooked as a vegetable before maturity. The yellow pollen harvested from mature flower heads can be used as a flour additive or added to soups and other foods as a nutrient/flavor boost. The pointy, lateral shoots emerging from rhizomes are tasty raw or cooked. Harvest while still whitish, before they curve upward to start new growth. Rhizomes can be harvested all winter and processed for the starch. One method is to peel off the skin and pound the root in water to produce a thick slurry; allow

Flowering stem shoots, and upper male (staminate) cattail spike with pollen

it to settle before pouring off the water. Add the slurry to soups, breads, etc. The root can also be peeled and cut into thin slices, dried thoroughly, then ground in a food processor or grain mill to produce a starch/fiber mixture. Put the mixture in a jelly bag suspended in a sealed jar and agitate to settle out the powder for use as a flour additive or substitute. Store until late summer when the pollen is available, then combine both with a bit of water. Form into patties and bake for tasty cattail cakes. The long leaves make good thatching for shelter or can be woven into mats, sandals, or hats/visors. Dried stalks make a serviceable hand-drill fire spindle. The fluffy seedhead fibers make good fire-starter, or stuff them between layers of clothing for emergency insulation.

Warnings/Comments: When harvesting rhizomes in winter, look for last year's flower heads to make sure they are cattails, not similar-appearing marsh plants. Leaf stalks should be mild flavored and roundish to oval, not flattened.

APPENDIX A: PLANTS BY FOOD TYPE

SALAD GREENS/FLOWERS/POTHERBS
(SPRING–EARLY SUMMER, LATE FALL)

Amaranth/lamb's quarter/saline saltbush (shoots, leaves)

Canada/wild onion (leaves, bulblets)

Cattail (shoots, leaf bases, pollen)

Chickweed (leaves)

Chicory (flowers, leaves)

Climbing false buckwheat/black bindweed (flowers, leaves)

Cut-leaved coneflower (shoots, flowers, leaves)

Dandelion (flowers, leaves)

Dayflower (flowers, leaves)

Devil's needles (leaves)

Eastern redbud (flowers, young seedpods)

Field sorrel (leaves, seeds)

Greenbrier (shoots, leaves)

Hedge mustard (leaves, seeds)

Lousewort (leaves, flowers)

Orange daylily (bases of leaves, young flower shoots, buds, flowers)

Oxeye daisy (leaves, buds, flowers)

Peppergrass/field cress (leaves, tops)

Pineapple weed (leaves, flowers)

Plains yucca (flowers)

Plantain (leaves, seeds)

Prairie parsley (shoots, leaves)

Purple poppy mallow (tops, flowers)

Purple/white prairie clover (leaves, flower buds)

Purslane (leaves, stems)

Redbud (flowers, leaves, seedpods)

Shepherd's purse (leaves, tops)

Smartweeds (leaves, flowers)

Spiderwort (flowers)

Spring beauty (leaves, flowers)

Violet (leaves, flowers)

Violet/yellow wood sorrel (leaves, flowers, seedpods)

Watercress (leaves, tops)

Whitemouth dayflower (leaves, flowers)

Wild carrot (leaves, flowers)

Wild lettuce (leaves)

Wild onion (leaves)

POTHERBS/VEGETABLES (LATE SPRING, SUMMER, FALL)

American lotus (unfurled leaves)

Beeplant (shoots, tops)

Chicory (leaves)

Common burdock (shoots, petioles)

Common mallow (leaves, flowers)

Common milkweed (shoots, seedpods)

Cup rosinweed (meristems, young leaves)

Curly dock (shoots, leaves)

Devil's claw (pods)

Evening/sand primrose (shoots, tops)

Goatsbeard (shoots, leaves, flowers)

Milkweed (shoots, flowers, seedpods)

Plains yucca (shoots, fruits)

Pokeweed (shoots, tops)

Prairie parsley/golden Alexanders (young shoots, tops)

Prickly pear (pads)

Reed canary grass (shoots)

Solomon's seal/false Solomon's seal
(shoots)
Sow thistle (leaves)
Spiderwort (shoots)
Thistles (peeled shoots, leaves, raw or
cooked)

Velvetleaf (shoots, tops, flowers)
Wintercress (shoots, tops, leaves)
Wood/stinging nettle (shoots, tops)
Yellow pond lily (unfurled or
underwater young leaves)

FRUIT/BERRIES (LATE SPRING–FALL)

American plum/sand plum/
chokecherry/sand cherry/black
cherry
Blackberry/black raspberry/dewberry
Buffalo pea
Buffaloberry
Elderberry
False Solomon's seal (fruits)
Gooseberry/buffalo currant

Ground cherry/black nightshade
Hackberry
Hawthorn
Prickly pear (fruit)
Red mulberry
River grape
Serviceberry/Saskatoon berry
Wild strawberry

SEEDS/BEANS (SUMMER–FALL)

Amaranths
Biscuitroot
Broad-leaved plantain
Buffalo gourd
Climbing false buckwheat/black
bindweed
Common mallow
Cup plant
Curly dock
Elms
Fuzzy bean
Hog peanut
Illinois bundleflower (green pods)
Lamb's quarter
Lotus/yellow pond lily/water lily

Marsh elder
Mustards
Prairie parsley
Prickly pear
Primrose
Purslane
Ragweed
Reed canary grass
Tall thistle
Velvetleaf
Wild bean (pods)
Wild carrot
Wood/stinging nettle
Yellow pond lily

BULBS/ROOTS/TUBERS (SOME SPRING OR WINTER ONLY)

American licorice
American lotus
Biscuitroot
Bush morning glory
Canada/wild onion

Cattail
Common arrowhead
Eastern camas
Evening/sand primrose
Goatsbeard

Groundnut
Hog peanut
Orange day lily
Purple poppy mallow
Reed canary grass
Spring beauty
Sunroot

Thistle
Timpsila
Wild carrot
Wild potato vine
Yellow nutsedge
Yellow pond lily

NUTS (LATE SUMMER-FALL)
Black walnut
Bur oak (acorns)

Hazelnut
Pecans/hickories

SEASONINGS
Horseweed
Mints
Peppergrass

Smartweed
Wild carrot (seeds)
Reed canary grass (roots for sugar)

TEAS AND BEVERAGES
Blackberry/black raspberry/strawberry
    (fruits, leaves)
Dandelion/chicory (flowers, roasted
    roots)
Leadplant
Lemon bee balm and other mints
New Jersey tea
Persimmon (leaves)

Pineapple weed
Reed canary grass (sweet stems)
Rosehips
Silver buffaloberry
Sumac berry
White avens (roasted roots)
Wood nettle
Yellow nutsedge (tubers)

APPENDIX B: GETTING STARTED

Learning to use wild foods is like any endeavor; the more time spent with it, the more useful it becomes. As with mushrooms, never be casual about identification when consuming foraged plants. **You can't have too many books on foraging and wildflower identification!** Regional books are always better. If you're on a tight budget, online used booksellers often sell used copies of some popular guides for less. If you're on social media, look for foraging groups to find local practitioners and events. Seek out and cultivate relationships with teachers and mentors, as our pre-technological ancestors did. Many state and federal parks and local organizations offer wildflower or edible plant walks and programs; these activities are great for expanding plant knowledge and meeting other people with similar interests. Plant or visit a garden and familiarize yourself with the edible "weeds" that pop up. Many of our weedy garden invaders were brought by early colonists from Europe and other countries because they were valued for food or medicine. Look for these common plants in disturbed ground, urban waste areas, and unmowed edges of untreated lawns and fields. The prairie region has many access points in the numerous national grasslands, state parks, private prairies, lakes, and other public lands, some of which offer naturalist-led programs. All are great places to learn about local plants. Driving backroads along pastures and open land will also turn up roadside goodies.

As mentioned in General Foraging Guidelines, all public lands have regulations about foraging, always check first. **Always watch where you put your hands and feet during outings!** Copperheads and rattlesnakes may be about, and you don't want your adventure to turn into an ER visit.

I learned to familiarize myself with plants by keeping wildflower field guides handy in accessible places, such as the coffee table next to the couch, the bed stand, and, of course, in the bathroom. Once you learn the Latin name of a plant, you can use the internet to find out what the rest of the world knows about it. The Biota of North America Project website (http://bonap.org) is a great tool to learn what species are found in your area. An internet search of the plant genus name followed by BONAP will give county-level occurrence maps for each species in the genus.

Tools and Equipment: Carry field guides, notebooks, and/or a smartphone (aka pocket outrage generator) in the field and use plant apps or take pics for later identification. Plant apps are getting better but are not completely reliable; confirm identification with multiple sources before consuming new species.

Tools needed for collecting are lightweight gloves, a small lock-blade or fixed-blade knife, and a digging tool if you are where root collecting is allowed. A stout walking stick is handy when navigating steep hills and rough country;

turn it into a digging stick by sharpening and fire-hardening the smaller end. Baskets are preferable for collecting, but reusable or plastic grocery bags can be folded up and carried easily in your pocket or backpack.

Kitchen tools: Use a molcajete, mano and metate, or mortar and pestle for grinding seeds/grains and pulverizing plants for pesto or bouillon. For softer roots and shoots, use a food mill. To harvest the pulp from soft fruits with seeds, use a cone ricer, chinois, or a wire mesh strainer. For processing crushed or processed roots for flour and nuts for milk, use milk nut bags or cheesecloth. If you are cooking where there is electricity, a heavy-duty blender such as a Vitamix, a good food processor, and a coffee grinder can make short work of some of the processing.

Preparing Your Harvest: Most plants can be used for stand-alone side dishes or combined with other ingredients for a main meal. Some plants may have strong or unique flavors that are unpalatable by themselves but can add zest to dishes with milder ingredients. Foraged foods may contain unfamiliar or strong flavors; keep in mind that our preferences have been conditioned by generations of selective breeding that has produced watery, sweet food crops. It's always fun to mix, match, and experiment to discover new and amazing combinations!

Salads: The average restaurant salad usually has four to six plant species. A wild-foraged spring salad may have ten to twenty or more species of greens and flowers in a mix of mild and strong flavors, providing a different taste combination in every bite. Students have commented that after tasting these salads, they won't go back to plain lettuce. Early fruits like wild strawberries and serviceberries are good additions, as are wild nuts and seeds. Toasted insects such as crickets or larvae provide a nutty-flavored salad topping, and they're cheaper than sunflowers seeds (see Appendix C: Edible Insects). Many spring greens will die back in the heat of summer then put out new growth with the cool and damp late-fall weather. While out hiking, carry a small bottle of balsamic or seasoned rice wine vinegar and a bit of seasoned salt. It's easy to throw together a great salad using a flat rock, a slab of dead wood, or a plastic collection bag for a bowl.

Potherbs: Cooking often improves texture, flavor, or edibility of wild greens. Plants such as curly dock may have bitter or tart flavors that are reduced by soaking in water overnight or cooking. Wood/stinging nettle has stinging hairs that are rendered harmless by cooking, and pokeweed greens contain toxins that need to be cooked off by one or more boilings. Some sturdier salad greens can also be cooked as potherbs and vegetables. Wilted greens can be made with the traditional vinegar and hot bacon grease, but there are many alternatives such as nut oils, lemon juice, seasoned rice wine, and balsamic or wild fruit vinegars.

Nuts: Hickory, walnut, and hazelnut can be dried in the shell after hulling and stored for several months. They are fine raw, but roasting often improves the flavor and lengthens shelf life during dry or frozen storage. The nuts can also be shelled and pickled in brine, but they will need to be thoroughly rinsed before use to remove some of the salt.

Seeds/Grains: Plant seeds can be sprouted or dried and stored in jars, then later roasted and ground for a flour additive for use in porridges, flatbreads, or seedcakes. Seedheads of grasses and sedges are an underutilized foraging resource! Pascal Baudar has written extensively about harvesting wild grains and seeds for consumption and may soon publish a book on the subject. Here are a few of his suggested extraction, processing, and winnowing methods:

1. Passive extraction by hanging the mature plants over a sheet or tarp and collecting what falls.
2. Extraction by using a grinder and/or rolling a rounded stone or pestle over the grains to remove the chaff.
3. Use a large bowl and a sort of racquet or beater to "slap" the plants and expel the seeds into the bowl.
4. Place seedpods in a plastic or paper bag and stomp on the bag to break the pods and release the seeds so they fall into the bottom of the bag. With smaller grains such as amaranth and lamb's quarter, put the tops inside a plastic bag then twist and shake till seeds fall out.
5. Remove the chaff by rubbing the seedheads in a circular motion between your hands.
6. Winnowing can be done by hand by blowing or using the wind to remove chaff. Another method is to put grains and chaff in a bowl and pour into another bowl in front of a small fan. Most winnowing methods take repeated effort to remove the chaff. Seeds and grains with softer exteriors such as curly dock can be ground whole for the extra fiber.

Fruits and Berries: Most fruits are best when eaten fresh, but many can be processed into fruit leathers, preserves, sauces, jellies, and syrups, dried whole, preserved in brandy, or pickled. Jellies usually require additional pectin, but some fruits contain it naturally. In my experience, low-sugar wild fruit syrups are far more useful than jams or jellies. Wild fruit syrups add amazing flavors when used as a sauce or drizzle for roasted or grilled meats and vegetables, desserts, and baked goods, and it can be added to vinaigrette dressings, cocktails, and other beverages. I prefer it to maple syrup on pancakes. Save your scraps after processing! Wild vinegars can be made easily with fruit skins and flesh still attached to seeds. Wild fruit syrups added to vinegars can produce very nice flavor combinations for vinaigrettes or fruit shrub drinks.

RECIPE

BASIC FRUIT SYRUP

Put fruits in a pan with enough water to cover, then heat or simmer to soften the flesh. Allow to cool, then work the flesh off the seeds. Strain through a wire mesh strainer to remove larger seeds; use cheesecloth to strain for smaller seeds. If needed, add a bit of sugar or sweetener to offset tartness, but not enough to overwhelm the fruit flavor. Reduce on low heat (keeping the heat below simmering temperature will help preserve vitamin C and volatile oils) until it reaches desired consistency, or add a small bit of fruit pectin for a shorter reduction time. Pour into small jars, refrigerate, and use within two to three months.

RECIPE

BASIC WILD FRUIT VINEGAR

Use scraps, fruits past their prime, skins, and seeds with remaining flesh after processing. Wild grapes, buffaloberries, wild plums/cherries, persimmons, and other large-seeded fruits used for jelly or syrup are preferred, but you can use any kind of fruit or berry.

Use these proportions or scale them up for larger batches: ⅓ cup sugar to 3–4 cups fruit or fruit scraps, about ⅓ cup apple cider vinegar with "mother" as a starter, and enough water to cover in a 2-quart jar. If fermentation doesn't start after three days, add champagne yeast. Fruit flies carry bacteria that can aid the process, so leave the container uncovered for a bit to let them have access and strain them out later. Other ingredients can be added, such as juniper berries, herbs, and anything else that will produce interesting flavors.

Make infused vinegars by adding anything that might produce a desirable flavor, such as aromatic herbs, twigs, roots and bulbs, pinecones and needles, and roasted oak or hickory bark.

Fruit Shrub Drinks: Use store-bought apple cider vinegar, homemade wild vinegar, or fire cider, then add plain or sparkling water sweetened with honey, maple syrup, fruit syrup, or your favorite sweetener till it achieves a tartness/sweetness ratio roughly to that of lemonade. Muddled or chopped fruit or berries are nice additions. For preservation, the mix should have around 5 percent acidity. These "drinking vinegars" were quite popular in sixteenth-century Europe and colonial America, and often combined with wines or spirits. It was a good way to kill bacteria in the water while preserving perishable summer fruit.

The switchel is also popular, made by mixing cider vinegar with water flavored with ginger root and sweetened with molasses. It can also be a fermented drink (ginger bug) by omitting the vinegar and adding champagne yeast to the water/molasses/ginger mixture.

Preservation: Easily preserve edible flowers, buds, seedpods, roots, shoots, and ripe or unripe fruits by placing them in leftover pickle juice. Seasoning herbs, seeds, and flavorful berries such as sumac can be dried in a dehydrator or oven on low heat and ground for later use. An old aluminum-frame storm window screen propped up flat on blocks with a small fan blowing across it can be used to dry large amounts of plant material or fungi. Freezing is a good option, but it may change the texture of some foods. Greens can be parboiled and frozen for later use. Many wild foods are great for pickling, lacto-fermenting, or canning, especially shoots, roots, flowers, and nuts. Many smaller fruits and berries can be frozen, or dried whole and stored in jars. Fleshier fruits with large seeds such as chokecherries and wild plums should be strained through a colander to remove skins and seeds. The remaining pulp can be frozen or spread thin on parchment or wax paper to dry for fruit leather. Pascal Baudar's books and social media posts are great for taking a deep dive into preservation, covering methods such as canning, pickling, salt-curing, alcohol preservation, lacto-fermentation, and other types of fermentation.

APPENDIX C: EDIBLE INSECTS

Insects are a regular part of the diet in many other countries, not as a survival food but because they taste great! In many countries, a variety of edible insect species can be found everywhere from street vendors to high-end restaurants. Toasted insects will add extra flavor and protein to your meal when snagged on your collecting forays. They contain as much or more protein per weight than meat, and insect larvae are rich in fat calories. Studies report that 20 percent of the world's population consumes insects in 80 percent of existing countries; it is the new frontier in sustainable food production.

Cook insects or larvae by toasting, boiling, or adding them to other cooked dishes. Generally, most bugs have a nutty flavor when toasted or cooked, and toasted larvae are especially delicious as a snack or salad topping. Common foraged insects include adult crickets (cricket flour is commercially available), grasshoppers, cicadas, dragonflies, mayflies, scorpions, spiders, and the larvae of wasps, ants, beetles, and acorn weevils. (Caution: Cockroaches, crickets, isopods [land shrimp], and many other terrestrial arthropods are related to shrimp and other crustaceans. Those with seafood allergies should avoid consuming them.) If your garden is ravaged by tomato hornworms or Japanese beetles, collect them to incorporate into your meals; recipes can be found online. Be prepared for surprises: The chemical that creates the "stink" of green stink bugs turns to pure delicious flavor when toasted. There is a festival called Jumil Day in Taxco, Mexico, that celebrates their food value and flavor. The flavor of wolf and orb weaver spiders is beefy and buttery when toasted, not at all what you'd expect!

Process most insects by removing legs and wings; adult insect legs can have tiny hooks and the wings burn easily. Some species of stinkbugs and other insects should be soaked in warm water before cooking to remove bitterness or possible toxins. Spiders can be cooked whole. Be bold and give it a try! If they don't taste good, don't eat them. Insects to avoid are centipedes, millipedes, and fuzzy caterpillars. Some of the larger adult beetles may have chemical defenses that make them taste bitter.

APPENDIX D:
INDUSTRIAL FOOD VS. WILD FOOD

Humans have been selecting the medicine and nutrition in our plant foods for over 10,000 years! Prior to agriculture, nomadic hunter-gatherers consumed hundreds of species representing dozens of plant families. Early farmers probably found that plants they had previously relied on didn't grow well outside their natural habitat, so they focused on species that would thrive in gardens. They later began to select for varieties that were larger, sweeter, and easier to process. These new garden foods may have been larger and better-tasting, but they also contained more sugar and water, and fewer vitamins, minerals, and nutrients than their wild counterparts. The resultant diet was considerably less varied and required more bulk to provide the same amount of nutrition of wild plants, while having fewer health-sustaining benefits.

Plants that required higher levels of processing and those with bitter flavors fell out of favor; those same bitter flavors were compounds had provided much of the medicinal benefits.

Recent archaeological studies confirm that Neolithic herder/farmers in those early agricultural communities were more susceptible to bone density loss, cavities, and various new diseases—and even grew physically shorter than their hunter-gatherer neighbors. A stable but less diverse food supply was apparently less beneficial to health than an intermittent but extremely varied food base.

Much of our current system relies on cultivating monocrops for their ease of mass production, marketability, and long shelf life, but these aspects can decrease nutritional quality. Croplands become exhausted of natural minerals and nutrients, requiring heavy use of fossil fuel–derived fertilizers and pesticides/herbicides. Long harvest-to-table times, loss of species variety, lack of genetic diversity in individual plants, reliance on grain-based and high-sugar foods, and yet-unknown impacts from genetic tampering are all factors in modern food production. These developments have produced a food source with considerably fewer health benefits than a diet including wild foods. Cumulatively, they may be contributing to common health problems such as plant allergies, diabetes, obesity, cancer, and other degenerative diseases.

In areas without available foraging opportunities or an abundance of wild-lands, there are still great alternatives to industrially grown food. Many areas are developing interconnected communities focused on healthy food awareness, which feature small-farm agritourism, farmers' markets with wider food selections than most supermarkets, and farm-to-table or wild-table dining opportunities offering wild species and organic, heirloom plant varieties. Some farms are now specializing in growing native and introduced wild plants for restaurants that offer wild fare on their menus.

GLOSSARY

REPRODUCTIVE STRUCTURE

Achene—A small, dry, one-seeded fruit that does not open to release the seed.

Anther—Pollen-containing part of a stamen.

Beak—A prominent pointed terminal projection of a seed or fruit.

Bract—A modified, usually small, leaflike structure often positioned beneath a flower or inflorescence, differing in shape or color from other leaves.

Calyx—A collective term for the sepals of one flower; the outer whorl of a flower, usually green.

Carpel—The female reproductive organ that encloses the ovules in the flowering plants.

Catkin—A flowering spike of trees or shrubs, typically downy, pendulous, composed of flowers of a single sex, and often wind pollinated.

Corolla—Collective term for the petals of a flower.

Cotyledon—The embryonic leaf or leaves in a seed, the first part to appear in a germinated seed.

Culm—The hollow stem of a grass or cereal plant that bears the flower.

Cyme—A flower cluster with a central stem bearing a single terminal flower that develops first, the other flowers in the cluster developing as terminal buds of lateral stems.

Dioecious—Male and female reproductive organs occur in separate individuals.

Disk floret—Any of a number of small tubular and usually fertile florets that form the central disk. They are often accompanied by ray florets and are commonly found in the family Asteraceae. In rayless flowers, the flower head is composed entirely of disk florets.

Drupe—A fleshy fruit with thin skin and a central stone containing the seed.

Inflorescence—The complete flower head of a plant, including stems, stalks, bracts, and flowers.

Keel—The bottom two fused petals of a flower, shaped like a boat keel; characteristic in some legumes.

Lenticels—Raised pores in a woody stem that allows gas exchange between the atmosphere and the plant's internal tissues.

Monoecious—Male and female reproductive organs occurring in the same individual.

Ovary—The enlarged basal portion of the pistil in the female organ of a flower; usually matures to a fruit.

Panicle—A loose branching cluster of flowers.

Pappus, or pappus bristles—A tuft of hairs on a fruit or seed.

Pedicel—A stem that attaches a single flower to the inflorescence, arising from a peduncle.

Peduncle—Main stalk of an inflorescence.

Petaloid—Resembling the petal of a flower.

Pistil—The female organs of a flower, comprising the stigma, style, and ovary.

Raceme—A flower cluster with the separate flowers attached by short equal stalks at equal distances along a central stem.

Rays, or ray florets—Radiating petals surrounding a disk floret, as in Asteraceae.

Sepal—Individual parts of a flower's calyx that encloses the petals; typically green and leaflike.

Silique—A slender, elongated seed capsule that splits into two halves at maturity, exposing several to many seeds.

Spike—An unbranched, indeterminate inflorescence in which the flowers are without stalks.

Stamen—The male organ of a flower, usually consisting of a stalk called the filament and a pollen-bearing anther.

Staminode—A flower with stamens but no pistil.

Stigma—The sticky stem of the pistil of the female reproductive system.

Style—A long, slender stalk that connects the stigma and ovary.

Tepal—One of the outer parts of a flower (collectively, the perianth). The term is used when these parts cannot easily be classified as either sepals or petals.

Umbel—An inflorescence in which a number of flower stalks or pedicels, nearly equal in length, spread from a common center.

Umbellet—A secondary umbel in a compound umbel, such as the carrot.

LEAF DESCRIPTIONS

Apex—Tip or uppermost part.

Axil—Upper angle between the stem and a leaf.

Basal rosette—Leaves forming a circle at the base of the stem and growing to a similar length, somewhat resembling the petals of a rose.

Bipinnate—Doubly pinnate; a compound leaf with individual leaflets that are pinnately divided.

Blade—Flattened part of a leaf.

Cauline—Leaves growing on the stem, usually the upper parts.

Ciliate—Pertaining to fringed fine hairs along a leaf margin.

Compound—A leaf with several leaflets; it usually detaches from the main stem at a node.

Crenate—Scalloped or having blunt or rounded teeth.

Crisped—Finely curled, as with the edges of leaves and petals.

Deltoid—Triangular; shaped like the Greek letter delta.

Dentate—Toothed or serrated.

Elliptic—Oval, with a short point or no point at the tip.

Entire—Leaf with smooth edges around the entire margin.

Lanceolate—Long and wider in the middle; shaped like a lance tip.

Ligule—In grasses, a membranous outgrowth at the junction of the leaf and leaf stalk. Ligule appearance can be diagnostic in some species.

Margin—Edge of a leaf blade.

Meristem—Topmost part of a shoot or bottom part of a root consisting of undifferentiated growth cells.

Node—Part of a stem where leaves or branches arise.

Oblanceolate—Much longer than wide and with the widest portion near the tip.

Obovate—Teardrop shaped; stem attaches to the tapering end.

Orbicular—Round, circular.

Ovate—Egg shaped or oval, with a tapering point and the widest portion near the petiole.

Ovate-acute—Ovate with a sharp tip.

Palmate—A compound leaf that is divided into leaflets whose stems emanate from a single central point.

Palmately lobed—A leaf that is divided into three or more distinct lobes, like the palm of a hand with outstretched fingers.

Peltate—A roundish leaf with the petiole connected at the center.

Petiole—A leaf stalk.

Pinnately compound—Having two rows of leaflets on opposite sides of the axil.

Pinnatifid—Pinnately divided or lobed, but not all the way to the central axis.

Rachis—Main stem of a pinnate leaf.

Reniform—Kidney shaped.

Serrate—Toothed, with asymmetrical teeth pointing forward; saw-toothed.

Sessile—Leaf attached directly to a stalk with no stem or petiole.

Sheath—The lower part of leaf enveloping the stem or culm.

Sinus—A notch or depression between two lobes or teeth on a leaf.

Spatulate—Spoon shaped, having a broad flat end that tapers to the base.

Ternately compound—A compound leaf with leaflets arranged in multiples of three.

GENERAL TERMS

Adventive—Introduced but not fully naturalized.

Angiosperm—A plant that produces flowers; seeds are enclosed within a hollow ovary. This group represents around 80 percent of all plants, including herbaceous plants, shrubs, grasses, and most trees.

Annual—Plant that completes its life cycle in one year.

Biennial—A plant that completes its life cycle within two years. It usually forms a basal rosette of leaves the first year, producing flowers and fruits the second year.

Corm—A fleshy, round stem base or tuber-like root used as a storage organ; usually covered with leafy scales.

Cosmopolitan—Worldwide distribution in appropriate habitats.

Mesic—A habitat with a moderate amount of moisture.

Perennial—Plants that go dormant over winter and regrow more than two years.

Rhizome (rhizomatous)—A perennial underground root or stem, usually growing horizontally.

Stolon—A slender, prostrate or trailing stem (runner) that produces roots and occasionally erect shoots at its nodes.

Xeric—A dry habitat with a low amount of moisture

INDEX

Bergamot, wild, 123, 157
Bergo, Alan, 60, 166, 172
Berries. *See also specific berries*
  harvest list, 214
  preparing, 218–220
Betulaceae, 69
Bidens bipinnata, 46–47
Bidens frondosa, 46, 47
Bidens spp., 46–47
Bigroot prickly pear, 77–79
Bindweeds, 86, 146
Biscuitroot, 4, 31–32
Bitternut, 118
Blackberry, 166, 168–169
Black bindweed, 146
Black cherry, wild, 164
Black hickory, 118
Black nightshade, 173–174
Black raspberry, 169
Black walnut, 120–121
Blaspheme vine, 209–210
Bluejacket, 201–202
Blue sailors, 62–63
Blue violet, common, 180–181
Bois d'Arc, 133
Brassicaceae, 70–76
Breadroot, 4, 110–112, 166
Broad-leaved dock, 150
Broad-leaved plantain, 11, 144–145
Broomrapes, 139
Broussonetia papyrifera, 134
Buckthorns, 157
Buckwheat, 146–147
Buffaloberry, 94–95
Buffalo currant, 116–117, 166
Buffalo gourd, 88–89
Bulbs, harvesting of, 5, 214–215
Bull thistle, 49
Burdocks, 43–45
Bur oak, 114–115
Bush morning glory, 86, 87

Buttercup, 60
Buttonweed, 126–127

Cactaceae, 77–79
"Cajun Coffee," 63, 66
Callirhoe alcaeoides, 128
Callirhoe digitata, 128
Callirhoe involucrate, 128–129
Camas, 8, 189, 191–193
Camassia angusta, 191
Camassia scilloides, 8, 191–193
Canada milkvetch, 101, 102
Canada onion, 188–190
Cannabaceae, 80–82
Capsella bursa-pastoris, 71–72
Carduus nutans, 49
Carolina false dandelion, 66
Carolina maygrass, 207
Carpenter dock, 60–61
Carrionflower, 209
Carrot, wild, 9, 29–30
Carrot-leaf desert parsley, 4, 31–32
Carya cordiformus, 118
Carya glabra, 118
Carya laciniosa, 118, 119
Carya ovata, 118, 119
Carya spp., 118–119
Carya texana, 118
Carya tomentosa, 118, 119
Caryophyllaceae, 83
Catbrier, 209–210
Cattail, common, 211–212
Ceanothus americanus, 157
Ceanothus herbaceus, 157
Celtis laevigata, 80
Celtis occidentalis, 80–82
Celtis reticulata, 80
Celtis tenuifolia, 80
Cerastium fontanum, 83
Cercis canadensis, 104–106, 181
Chamomile, 58